The New York Times

CHANGING PERSPECTIVES

Marijuana

EDUCATIONAL PUBLISHING BOOKS

THE NEW YORK TIMES EDITORIAL STAFF

Published in 2019 by The New York Times® Educational Publishing in association with The Rosen Publishing Group, Inc.
29 East 21st Street, New York, NY 10010

First Edition

The New York Times
Alex Ward: Editorial Director, Book Development
Phyllis Collazo: Photo Rights/Permissions Editor
Heidi Giovine: Administrative Manager

Rosen Publishing
Megan Kellerman: Managing Editor
Jacob R. Steinberg: Editor
Greg Tucker: Creative Director
Brian Garvey: Art Director

Cataloging-in-Publication Data
Names: New York Times Company.
Title: Marijuana / edited by the New York Times editorial staff.
Description: New York : New York Times Educational Publishing, 2019. | Series: Changing perspectives | Includes glossary and index.
Identifiers: ISBN 9781642821499 (library bound) | ISBN 9781642821482 (pbk.) | ISBN 9781642821505 (ebook)
Subjects: LCSH: Marijuana abuse—Juvenile literature. | Marijuana—Juvenile literature.
Classification: LCC HV5822.M3 M375 2019 | DDC 613.8'35—dc23

Manufactured in the United States of America

On the cover: Cannabis (marijuana) plants growing inside a flower room at the River Rock Medical Marijuana Center in Denver, Colo.; Matthew Staver for The New York Times.

Contents

Introduction

STRICTLY SPEAKING, cannabis is the name of a genus of plants used for a variety of industrial uses (hemp) and medical and recreational uses (marijuana). Perspectives on the legitimacy of the latter have varied greatly through the decades, but today, a trend toward the legalization and scientific study of cannabis is growing. As such, the history of cannabis and our perspectives on it merit attention to separate fact from fiction and to understand from where these perspectives originate.

American cultural attitudes toward marijuana in the late nineteenth and early twentieth centuries associated the drug with Mexican and Latino culture. In a Jan. 6, 1901, article titled "Doctors of Ancient Mexico," a New York Times correspondent described the effects of marijuana as a "long, deathlike sleep." The United States government demanded greater cooperation from its Mexican counterpart in policing the border and destroying cannabis crops in both countries.

By the 1930s, the American public feared cannabis. This attitude was spurred on by pleas to parents to fight a war against the drug and a popular 1936 propaganda film, "Reefer Madness," in which a group of high school students lured to try marijuana engage in a series of dangerous crimes.

Crime statistics and early medical research disproved a lot of the myths surrounding cannabis's effects on users, but the passage of the Marihuana Tax Act of 1937 made its cultivation, possession, importation and distribution regulated and expensive, curbing medical studies and fueling police raids and demonstrations in which confiscated cannabis was publicly burned.

In the 1960s, however, cultural attitudes began to shift as the counterculture came to reject establishment values, and Bohemian scenes

JIM WILSON/THE NEW YORK TIMES

The flowering buds of the cannabis plant are often ground and smoked, though a variety of preparations exist for both recreational and medicinal use of marijuana.

flourished in large urban centers. The beatniks and hippies of the 1960s opposed the Vietnam War and supported the Civil Rights Movement and the women's liberation movement, and many experimented with marijuana and lysergic acid diethylamide (LSD). The values of the counterculture became pervasive on college campuses, and marijuana became increasingly common among affluent youth.

In 1970, the cultural embrace of cannabis met its enemy in the Nixon administration, which declared drug abuse "public enemy number one" and sought to combat the distribution of cannabis and other substances via the Comprehensive Drug Abuse Prevention and Control Act of 1970. The act made cannabis a Schedule I drug, claiming it had no legitimate medical use and was prone to abuse. In 1973, the Drug Enforcement Agency was created to enforce these regulations.

Throughout the 1980s and '90s, the United States continued to engage in a costly war on drugs consisting of foreign aid to governments battling drug cartels, education campaigns focused on deterring schoolchildren and teenagers from trying drugs, and the incarceration of drug traffickers.

Beginning in the late 1990s and continuing until today, states have gradually embraced the legalization of cannabis, initially for only medicinal use but more recently for recreational use as well. Federal classification of cannabis has not changed, though enforcement has been inconsistent in the face of growing legalization in individual states and more relaxed cultural attitudes.

Today, as cannabis becomes increasingly available and its use less stigmatized, studies of the beneficial and adverse effects of its use are changing our understanding of its potential. One risk previously unidentified is cannabinoid hyperemesis syndrome, a condition triggered by heavy cannabis use and characterized by recurrent vomiting and nausea. Though cured by abstinence, the adverse effects observed in patients suffering from the syndrome stand in sharp contrast to its therapuetic effects in patients with cancer or other chronic illness.

On the cultural front, the social justice movement has brought attention to the widely varying discrepancies in arrest and incarceration rates based on race as well as the big money behind the private prison system, which is heavily invested in increasing prison population size.

Now, as several states (such as California, Washington and Colorado, to name a few) and Canada have made recreational marijuana legal, cannabis is a multibillion-dollar business, and it would seem the tide would be difficult to turn back.

The articles that follow bear witness to the changing perspectives on cannabis through the ages and offer various lenses through which to view the current trend toward legalization and its impact. While this trend is still developing, much research is yet to be done on the long-term effects of cannabis and the full scope of its applications.

CHAPTER 1

1900s–50s: Americans Fear "Reefer Madness"

In the first half of the twentieth century, Americans predominantly associated cannabis with Mexico and Latin American immigrants. This belief manifested in racist attitudes toward Latinos in the United States and demands for tighter border patrol on the Mexico-United States border. In these decades, the first laws were passed classifying cannabis as a narcotic and establishing sentences for its trafficking, though sentencing varied vastly from state to state. Meanwhile, medical researchers began to study the risks and possible benefits of cannabis use.

Poison Put in Cigarettes

BY THE NEW YORK TIMES | MAY 10, 1914

DR. F. LEROY SILVEY of Tuxpam, Mexico, now at the McAlpin here in New York, explained last night the significance of the Mexican officer's explanation of the madness of Private Parks. Lieut. Col. Taggart went to the Mexican lines and asked about his orderly. The Mexican officer would not admit that Parks had been killed, but answered: "Maybe your man smoked a poisoned cigarette. Mexican women in Vera Cruz give them to men and they always go crazy."

"I have seen several Americans in the same demented condition," said Dr. Silvey. "It is the result of smoking marajuana, one of the most mysterious and deadly drugs I have ever seen. The Mexican women mix the weed with tobacco and make cigarettes of the combination. It only takes a few to affect a man's brain seriously.

"One case in particular I remember because I foolishly thought that I could cure the man. An oil driller became infatuated with a Mexican girl. It lasted for a time and then he began to get over it. She noticed that she was losing him and went to the older women and asked how she could keep him. They gave her some marajuana cigarettes and she gave them to him to smoke. The native tobacco is bitter and one cannot notice the taste of the marajuana. I ran across the man after he had smoked the drug and the change was awful. I treated him with everything I knew for some time, but it was hopeless.

"I do not know what the drug is. I smoked just a taste of a marajuana cigarette for the sake of experiment. It acted on me like the strongest narcotic and I could feel it in my head for a week. Needless to say I never tried it again."

Mexico to Join U.S. in Fight on Drugs

BY JOSEPH DE COURCY | MAY 10, 1925

MEXICO CITY, MAY 4 — The drug treaty which will be formulated in El Paso by the Commissioners of the United States and representatives of the Mexican Government is expected to achieve two results — elimination of the constant stream of drugs which is pouring into the United States through Mexico and help to clean out from the border towns several groups of American and foreigners who have made large sums of money through the drug traffic.

Charles Beecher Warren, when special Ambassador of the United States to Mexico, learning of the tremendous amount of drugs that were being shipped from Europe and Asia to Mexico for transhipment to the United States, suggested to Washington that an agreement be reached with the Mexican Government in the form of a treaty which would permit the cooperation of the police officials of both countries to suppress this traffic and to punish the drug dealers.

Mr. Warren's departure for the United States caused those plans to fall through until the arrival of Ambassador James Rockwell Sheffield. One of the first official acts of the new Ambassador was to propose to the Mexican Government the advisability of a drug and immigration treaty which would lessen crime along the border and remove a sore spot which has caused friction between the two countries.

President Calles, in an effort to clean up Mexico City, issued orders to the Police Department to round up all drug users and dealers. To date police have discovered over twenty shops where drugs were sold at retail and have captured three leaders of the native drug gangs. Five saloons where drugs were sold over the bar have been closed and the owners are now awaiting trial.

One American saloon keeper was arrested and deported to San Francisco, where he is now serving out an uncompleted term in prison. The capture of drugs in his saloon started a search into his past history, resulting in finding that he had escaped from San Francisco while out on bail.

President Calles has stated all Americans found engaged in drug traffic will be immediately deported and placed in the hands of the American authorities.

President de la Huerta, in the six months that he was in office, started an investigation into the rumors that Mexico was being used as a base for drugs and that a number of minor officials were implicated in drug smuggling. A commission was appointed by de la Huerta to work under cover. The reports of this commission, which made a complete investigation, reached so high in official circles that de la Huerta was forced to admit that he was unable to proceed, as the assistance of these officials was needed in consolidating the Administration which was trying to bring about harmony between the Obregon followers and the ex-followers of the dead President Carranza.

DRUG TRAFFIC IN MEXICAN PORTS

Reports showed that the Atlantic coast ports were being used as ports of entry for drugs purchased in Germany, France and Belgium. German steamers invariably bring drugs. Members of the crew, it is stated by shipping men, have been known to pay for the privilege of working as seamen in order to bring drugs to Tampico, Vera Cruz, Tlacotalpam and Puerto Mexico. It is also stated in reports that officers of certain ships always bring packages of drugs, which are disposed of in these ports. Tampico, with its cosmopolitan crowds, offers unusual opportunities to drug importers to get rid of drugs at high prices. Saloons run by Americans and Spaniards, hotels of the lower types and also a group of adventurers are always willing to handle anything that promises large returns. Numbers of oil workers, returning from the fields with several months' wages unspent, fall an easy prey to drug dealers in cheap saloons.

Small quantities of drugs are carried across the border in pigskin coverings. These packages, similar in shape to a sausage, are carried concealed on the body and unless the inspectors are suspicious and make a complete search by stripping the carrier naked, they are carried into the cities where the drugs are distributed. Several dealers come to Mexico from cities as far north as St. Louis and Chicago.

The discovery by the Mexican Government of several hundred acres of cultivated poppies in the States of Nayarit and Durango give rise to the belief that the west coast of Mexico produces many hundred kilos of opium unknown to the Government. The fields that were located were being cultivated by a group of Chinese who confessed that they extracted opium from these plants. Orders have been issued by the Federal Government to wipe out these fields. The question now arises: Can the Government force the Chinese to abandon the cultivation of poppies?

Acapulco and Salina Cruz on the west coast of Mexico are favorite landing places for opium and kindred drugs coming from Japan and the East. Japanese steamers touch at these ports and carry supplies for the dealers. Quantities of opium are smuggled ashore from these steamers and shipped into Mexico City, passing through the isthmus of Tehuantepec to Vera Cruz, then to Mexico. Drug dealers have their agents in these ports.

Japanese fishermen of the west coast of Lower California are also said to be engaged in the drug traffic. It is stated by investigators that the fishermen have an agreement with the steamers which carry supplies of drugs to be sold in California. Buoys loaded with drugs are dropped from the steamer when it reaches a certain point near the Lower California coast. Fishermen sailing to the fishing grounds make an extra leg to deep water, locate the buoy with drugs, then sail to the fishing ground. The drugs are landed by being stuffed into certain fish which are carefully marked. They are taken to the homes of the fishermen and then transferred to the agents of the dealers who ship the drugs into California.

Mexico City dailies have featured several times stories that certain business houses of the city have permits to import quantities of drugs from Europe. Names have been freely given of houses that have sold drugs legally, but the press has shown that if drugs enter Mexico with such facility that houses which are supposed to be devoted to selling furniture and clothes can change into drug importing houses, then the law must be amended so that the drug traffic will be restricted to the amount that is really needed for medical use.

One of the choice scandals published in the local press was the exposure of the representative of a Central America country who purchased a quantity of drugs from one of these business houses and then shipped the drugs to Central America without permission of the Mexican Government. An investigation was started which resulted in finding that this representative had made a number of similar shipments. His recall was requested by the Mexican Government, which placed all the facts in the case at the disposal of his Government.

El Universal published a letter from a Mexican signed El Rubio, dated Douglas, Ariz., addressed to a former Chief of Police of Mexico City who is now in jail awaiting trial. The letter stated the writer had a market for four hundred grams of cocaine, heroin and morphine and was anxious for a shipment to be made at once. Colonel Barcenas, present Chief of Police of Mexico City, immediately advised the American authorities of the address of this drug agent in Arizona.

One of the features of the proposed treaty will deal with the growing of marihuana, Mexican hashish, which is cultivated in Mexico and also in the southern part of the United States. The Mexican Government has prohibited the cultivation of marihuana, but as one small plant will give enough leaves to make a number of cigarettes it is difficult to prevent the cultivation. In Texas, according to a press report, there is no law which prevents the cultivation of marihuana.

The Mexican people are heartly backing the proposed treaty, as they have seen the results of the drug traffic as causes of a number of revolting crimes committed by drug addicts.

Mexican officials have expressed desires actively to cooperate with the American authorities in not only suppressing the evil but also in capturing dealers in order to punish them with a term in jail, as they realize that in the trail of the drug smuggler are the bribers, dive keepers, and all sorts of criminals.

Marijuana Smoking Is Reported Safe

BY THE NEW YORK TIMES | NOV. 21, 1926

PANAMA, NOV. 14 — A Panaman Judge recently sentenced an American seaman, Hamilton Main, to a year of penal confinement for smoking and having in his possession cigarettes made of the leaves of the cannabis indica, known also as marijuana, canjac and by various other names, and often incorrectly referred to as hashish.

About a year ago there was considerable comment on the fact that this weed was being grown in the public parks of New York City by a group said to be Mexicans. Sunday newspaper features are still being printed about the fearful consequences of using this allegedly habit-forming and dreadful weed.

An investigation made by a special committee appointed by Colonel M. L. Walker, Governor of the Panama Canal, raises grave doubts as to the effects produced by smoking marijuana. The committee was composed of Colonel W. P. Chamberlain, Chief Health Officer; F. E. Mitchell, District Attorney; Guy Johannes, Chief of Police; and C. H. Calhoun, head of the Customs Service, assisted by L. B. Bates, Chief of the Ancon Hospital Laboratory; Dr. George E. Hesner, Superintendent of the Corozal Hospital for the Insane; Colonel William B. Rigby, Judge Advocate General, U. S. A., Panama Canal Department, and Surgeon E. H. H. Old, U. S. N.

LITERATURE WAS STUDIED

The investigation took the form of studying available literature on the subject, writing to the authors for sources of information and actual experiment with subjects smoking marijuana, which is the Latin-American name for the hemp and is probably a combination of the names Mary and Jane in Spanish, Maria y Juana.

Some articles by men of supposed scientific knowledge were based on sources other than actual experiment, and the authors of some apparently learned monographs on the use of marijuana had never seen a subject under the influence of the weed, nor did they know of first-hand knowledge of the dire results alleged to lie due to its use, according to the committee.

"While anybody can gather the plant and prepare it for use, it is sold more or less openly already made up," a recent Sunday feature story in an American newspaper said.

"Mixed with tobacco, or made 'straight' into a cigarette, a few puffs are enough to send the smoker into the realm of half-dream, half-reality."

Speaking of the "plight of Kansas" this article said:

> *School children are smoking it, prisoners are growing it secretly in the jail yards, grown-ups soak it in perfume. Scores have already gone crazy from it and hundreds are getting that way as fast as they can.*

The weed, really Indian hemp, came up for discussion at the Geneva conferences on narcotics. Chapter XIX of "Opium as an International Problem," a book by Professor W. W. Willoughby of Johns Hopkins University, carries the title "Indian Hemp (Hashish)," and gives a résumé of what was done on the subject at the conference.

MIXED WITH OTHER MATERIALS

The question was brought up by M. El Guindy, the Egyptian delegate, who referred to the "cannabis indica or sativa as hashish." He explained that hashish was used in the form of a paste made from the resin of the flowers, mixed with sugar and cooked with butter and aromatic substances, the resulting concoction being known in Egypt by the names of "manzul, maagun and garawish." It was also cut into small fragments and mixed with tobacco for smoking in cigarettes, or simply smoked in hookahs, he said.

Apparently M. El Guindy made no distinction between the use of the hemp as a part of the paste known as "manzul ect," and as a weed for smoking either pure or mixed with tobacco.

Of the effects he said:

> *Taken in small doses, hashish at first produces an agreeable inebriation, a sensation of well-being and a desire to smile; the mind is stimulated. A slightly stronger dose brings a feeling of depression and of discomfort. There follows a kind of hilarious and noisy delirium in persons of a cheerful disposition, but the delirium takes a violent form in persons of violent character. The habitual use of hashish brings on chronic hashishism. The addict very frequently becomes neurasthenic and eventually insane.*

CANAL TESTS MADE BY SMOKING

The experiments carried out in the Canal Zone were confined to the smoking of the weed, some of which was cultivated in the plant introduction gardens of the Panama Canal, some collected from wild plants, but all properly identified. It may be pointed out that the effects reported from the use of some of the concoctions of which marijuana is a component part may have resulted from the other ingredients.

The most thorough study of the subject in the investigations was that of Dr. M. V. Ball of Warren, Pa., the results of which were published in the Journal of the American Medical Association under the title "The Effects of Hashish Not Due to Cannabis Indica."

Cannabis indica, according to one member of the commission, seems to have got into bad company, and it is the association with other drugs that has brought an undeserved reputation to marijuana.

"It seems to me," writes Dr. Ball, "that all the symptoms ascribed to the use of cannabis indica are to be explained by the admixtures which are ordinarily contained in the hemp preparations as they appear in the ganja shops and the hashish joints of the Oriental countries. There is no record to my knowledge of any habitués of cannabis indica among the Anglo-Saxons."

Ganja is one of the forms in which the hemp is used in India, although always with other ingredients, and on this subject the Indian Hemp Commission, which made a thorough study of the subject for the British Government, reported in part:

The alleged cases of insanity due to ganja smoking were for the most part not clearly proved; those who indulged in crime were not driven to it by excessive use of this drug, but when excesses were noted they were usually connected with other vices, such as alcohol and opium. Not a single medical witness could clearly prove that the habit gave rise to mental aberration.

SEVENTEEN SUBJECTS TOOK PART

Seventeen subjects smoked marijuana during the course of the investigation made in the Canal Zone. All were under competent and careful medical observation. In two investigations twelve volunteers smoked from two to twelve cigarettes of marijuana. Only one experienced the effects of incoordination and mental confusion. In the report of the test made of two soldiers about twenty years of age, who said that they were more or less habitual smokers of the weed, it is stated:

Both soldiers said that the smoke from the drug tasted the same as the smoke from the plant which they had been accustomed to smoking, and that they felt fully as much effect or "kick" from it as they usually did. This they described as a feeling of lightness and of happiness. However, their general conduct and behavior appeared perfectly normal. Each had a very dry throat and mouth and a slight increase in pulse rate, and — face was somewhat flushed. They had perfect coordination and showed no other signs either mental or physical.

Each of these men smoked six marijuana cigarettes in a little more than one hour.

SMOKED IT FROM CHILDHOOD

Three soldiers were the subjects of a later test, and one of them, a man of 25, from Texas, said he had smoked marijuana since he was a child 7 or 8. He declared he had no craving for marijuana and did not think it habit-forming. He felt no ill effects from it the following day and did not think it had ever done him any harm, he said.

Another had been smoking marijuana for a little more than a year, sometimes smoking it every day and at other times going for quite a while without it. He does not crave it and does not think it is habit forming. He prefers tobacco.

The third said that he had been smoking marijuana every three or four days for about a year, from one to three cigarettes at a time, and that he felt the effect from the first cigarette, but preferred tobacco.

He said he could not describe the effect produced, but that "time flies, and it puts you in a sleepy condition." Once in a while it produced no effect whatever. This subject smoked three cigarettes within an hour and no appreciable effects were noticed.

The subject who had used marijuana from childhood showed moderate reaction after smoking four cigarettes, and could not walk a chalk line, his left foot usually being out of line. However, he showed fair coordination in hands and arms.

The third subject smoked four cigarettes and at no time did he show any effect from smoking the drug.

Incidentally, two of these subjects had qualified as marksmen and the one who had smoked the weed since childhood had qualified as an expert marksman.

REPORTS EFFECTS EXAGGERATED

The committee, in reporting to the Governor of the Panama Canal, stated:

> *The influence of the drug when used for smoking is uncertain and appears to have been greatly exaggerated. The reports seem to have little basis in fact, and there is no medical evidence that it causes insanity. Tests conducted by our local board confirm the evidence that the plant is not a habit-forming drug, and no pleasurable sensations nor acts of violence were observed. The board concluded that there is no evidence that the marijuana grown locally is a habit-forming drug in the sense of the term as applied to alcohol, opium, cocaine, &c., or that it has any appreciable deleterious effect on the individuals using it.*

The board recommended that no steps be taken by the authorities of the Canal Zone to prevent the sale or use of marijuana, and that no special legislation on that subject was needed.

In some States of the United States, California being one, marijuana is classed with cocaine, heroin, opium and other dangerous narcotic drugs, and penalties are applied for violation of the regulations governing its use.

It is realized that the experiments in the Canal Zone were limited and not conclusive, as they were made only on Anglo-Saxons.

Use of Marijuana Spreading in West

BY THE NEW YORK TIMES | SEPT. 16, 1934

DENVER, SEPT. 13 — Although as appalling in its effects on the human mind and body as narcotics, the consumption of marijuana appears to be proceeding, virtually unchecked in Colorado and other Western States with a large Spanish-American population. The drug is particularly popular with Latin Americans and its use is rapidly spreading to include all classes.

The poisonous weed which maddens the senses and emaciates the body of the user, is being sold more or less openly in pool halls and beer gardens throughout the West and Southwest and, according to some authorities, it is being peddled to school children. The Federal Government is powerless to stop the traffic, officials of the Narcotic Bureau say, because marijuana was left out of the Harrison Act under which the bureau gets its authority to stop the traffic in opium and its derivatives.

The seriousness of the problem, growing out of laxity in enforcing State laws barring the drug, is indicated by the fact that it is the same weed from which the Egyptian hashish is made. The plant grows wild in many parts of the United States, but when cultivated it is usually concealed in a stand of some other high-growing crop such as sugar beets, alfalfa or corn. After it grows to a height of three or four feet it blossoms and is cut and dried. The leaves and blossoms are then packed in ordinary pocket-size tobacco tins which retail at $3 to $5 each and contain enough "hay" to make thirty or forty cigarettes, one of which is enough to intoxicate the smoker.

The sensations of the addict are wholly different from those of the user of narcotics. Users of marijuana become stimulated as they inhale the drug and are likely to do anything. Most crimes of violence in this section, especially in country districts, are laid to users of the drug. However, it is said that the marijuana habit can be more easily broken than that of narcotics.

The weed's toxic qualities are not confined to men, but have equally deleterious effects on animals. Kin to the loco weed, marijuana when mixed with hay causes death to the horses that eat it.

Quotas

LETTER TO THE EDITOR | BY C. M. GOETHE | SEPT. 15, 1935

MARIHUANA, perhaps now the most insidious of our narcotics, is a direct by-product of unrestricted Mexican immigration. Easily grown, it has been asserted that it has recently been planted between rows in a California penitentiary garden. Mexican peddlers have been caught distributing sample marihuana cigarettes to school children. Mexico maintains a quota against us. Bills for our quota against Mexico have been blocked mysteriously in every Congress since the 1924 Quota Act. Our nation has more than enough laborers. We are supporting millions on the dole. Why should we not enact against Mexico the same quota we have against Great Britain, Germany, Scandinavia, Italy?

C. M. GOETHE, Sacramento, Calif.

War on Marihuana Urged on Parents

BY THE NEW YORK TIMES | MAY 4, 1937

RICHMOND, VA., MAY 3 — Relentless warfare on marihuana, which was termed the latest narcotic menace to youth, was urgently recommended to the National Congress of Parents and Teachers here today by Mrs. Hamilton Wright, special representative of the Federal Bureau of Narcotics. The congress opened its convention this morning with 2,000 members present.

Addressing a group on the use of alcohol and narcotics, one of a series of afternoon conferences on a variety of problems to be held throughout most of the week, Mrs. Wright characterized marihuana as the "most pernicious" of drugs.

She said it produced in smokers of the weed a temporary sense of complete irresponsibility which led to sex crimes and other "horrible" acts of violence.

Comparatively few persons are familiar with it, she explained, because it was introduced into the country ten years ago as a cigarette by Mexican peddlers, who have since reaped a financial harvest on its sale in the larger centers. But in that short time, she added, every State save South Carolina, Kentucky and Tennessee had passed laws against it.

At the opening session Dr. John W. Studebaker, Federal Commissioner of Education, told the delegates that one major task of education today was to "teach youth to think clearly, reason, weigh evidence and enable them to meet new situations."

He followed Mrs. B. F. Langworthy of Chicago, retiring president of the congress, who pleaded for the abolition of "such forces for corruption as the tavern, where young people may buy liquor."

Mrs. J. K. Bettingill of Detroit, first vice president, was nominated as Mrs. Langworthy's successor. Balloting on new officers will be held tomorrow.

At the general session tonight, Dr. Forrest E. Long, Professor of Education, New York University, discussed the question, "What is a Literate Community?"

Late in the afternoon the delegates were received at the Executive Mansion by Governor and Mrs. Beery.

Vocational guidance is more needed in schools than vocational education, according to Dr. Studebaker.

"The education for most vocations," he said, "is relatively easy compared to the task of finding one's work in this day of baffling complexities. Certainly children and young people ought to be given guidance at various stages in their educational experience which will help them to explore intelligently the various vocational fields."

Dr. Studebaker said the starting of processes of self-government in schools was one of the "most progressive developments" in modern education.

Mrs. Langworthy not only denounced taverns where youth may have access to liquor, but also pool rooms where "slot machines and other forms of gambling are permitted, soft drink parlors with curtained booths, moving picture houses with low grade pictures and 'bank nights.' " She commended support of such agencies as Boy and Girl Scouts, Camp Fire Girls, the Y. M. C. A. and Y. W. C. A.

Bettie Allen Thomas of Washington, representing Allied Youth, Inc., said in the conference on alcohol and narcotics that youngsters should not merely be taught the dangerous effects of alcohol but should be shown by practical programs that social pleasures and "getting along in one's position are not dependent upon the social cocktail or other drink."

Mrs. Jennie E. Nichols, national chairman, told the conference on humane education that crimes of violence, such as lynching, could be curtailed in a few generations by teaching children to be humane.

Physical defects are frequently responsible for the fact that some children appear unintelligent, Mrs. John S. Gibbons of Coral Gables, Fla., said in a discussion of the "exceptional child." She suggested the members could do a service to their communities by reporting cases of physical defects noted in neighborhood children.

The conference, at the suggestion of Mrs. Sue Stuart Brame of Jackson, Miss., will recommend to the National Board of Managers that Congress be asked to indorse a bill pending in the Senate to provide an annual appropriation of $11,580,000 for all types of physically handicapped children.

Experts Discount Marijuana as Big Factor in Crime but Drive on It Will Be Pressed

BY THE NEW YORK TIMES | JAN. 12, 1945

STUDIES BY THE Committee on the Marijuana Problem in the City of New York, appointed by Mayor La Guardia in January, 1939, have led the committee to the conclusion that "the practice of smoking marijuana does not lead to addiction in the medical sense of the word," that the drug is "not the determining factor in the commission of major crimes" and "is not widespread among school children," as some alarmist had reported, and that "juvenile delinquency is not associated with the practice of smoking marijuana."

Other conclusions in the 220-page report, published by the Jaques Cattell Press, Lancaster, Pa., and made public yesterday by the Mayor, follow.

Marijuana is used extensively in the Borough of Manhattan but the "problem is not as acute as it is reported to be in other sections of the United States."

The introduction of marijuana into this area is recent as compared to other localities.

The cost of marijuana is low and therefore within the purchasing power of most persons; the distribution and use of marijuana is centered in Harlem; the majority of marijuana smokers are Negroes and Latin Americans; the consensus among the marijuana smokers is that "the use of the drug creates a definite feeling of adequacy."

Further findings are that "the sale and distribution of marijuana is not under the control of any single organized group"; that its use "does not lead to morphine or heroin or cocaine addiction" and that "the publicity concerning the catastrophic effects of marijuana smoking in New York City is unfounded."

In the introduction to the report the Mayor says that "the findings are to be interpreted only as a reassuring report of progress and not as encouragement to indulgence, for I shall continue to enforce the laws prohibiting the use of marijuana until and if complete findings may justify an amendment to existing laws. The scientific part of the research will be continued in the hope that the drug may prove to possess therapeutic value for the control of drug addiction."

The studies were carried out through a committee of physicians, psychologists, sociologists and pharmacologists appointed by the Public Health Relations Committee of the New York Academy of Medicine and supported financially with grants of $7,500 each provided by the Commonwealth Fund, the Friedsam Foundation and the New York Foundation. Members of the Narcotic Squad of the New York Police Department helped materially in the studies.

Marijuana Traffic Is on the Increase

BY THE NEW YORK TIMES | JAN. 31, 1945

WASHINGTON, JAN. 30 — An increase in the traffic in marijuana, reappearance of heroin in moderate quantities and a decline in opium seizures during 1944 were reported today by the Treasury Department.

Agents of the department found evidence indicating that New York City was the focal point of the traffic in marijuana and four major gangs supplying the city were broken up, according to Elmer L. Irey, coordinator of enforcement. He reported that the traffic in some instances reached "the proportion of well-financed national and international conspirators."

The department disclosed that one of the New York gangs which came under investigation was the "107th Street Mob," formerly headed by "Lucky" Luciano. The investigation resulted in the indictment of seventeen persons in New York.

The Treasury agents discovered that the major source of supply of the gang was Mexican opium and heroin and that the New Yorkers were dealing with members of the old Black Toni Parmagini gang in California, and investigations were extended to the West Coast. A number of smugglers, including Willie Levin, former partner of Parmagini and just released from a seventeen-year prison sentence, were captured.

Large quantities of marijuana were seized in the raids in New York, according to the Treasury's report. Other joint narcotic-customs investigations resulted in the breaking up of large drug-smuggling gangs operating through Phoenix and Nogales, Ariz., and one channeling dope from El Paso, Tex., to New Jersey.

High Court Backs Tax on Marihuana

BY THE NEW YORK TIMES | NOV. 14, 1950

WASHINGTON, NOV. 13 — The Supreme Court ruled unanimously today that a Federal tax might be valid, even though it was regulatory in effect and bore "close resemblance to a penalty."

At issue was the Government's tax of $100 an ounce on unlicensed sales of marijuana, a drug used legally for medicinal purposes, but sold widely, though illegally, for use as a narcotic in cigarettes. Justice Tom C. Clark delivered the court's opinion, overruling District Judge John P. Barnes of Chicago.

Judge Barnes had dismissed a Federal suit to collect $8,701.65 in marihuana taxes from Maria Melitona Sanchez and Armand Mota. The judge agreed with the defendants that the tax was not really a tax, but a penalty, inflicted without a hearing. He found it unconstitutional.

However, the Supreme Court decided "the tax in question is a legitimate exercise of the taxing power despite its collateral regulatory purpose and effect."

The Marijuana Tax Law imposes a tax ranging from $1 to $24 on any person importing, making, distributing or selling the drug in any form. Such persons must also register with the Bureau of Internal Revenue. Treasury orders must accompany each transfer of marijuana, subject to a tax of $1 an ounce.

But anyone who buys or sells the drug without registering or paying the registration tax is subject to a tax of $100 an ounce. And if the buyer does not pay the levy, the seller, or "transferor" is held responsible. Mrs. Melitona and Mr. Mota, were described as "transferors" of the drug.

Justice Clark conceded the imposition of a "severe burden" on sales by unlicensed persons represented an attempt by Congress to restrict the marijuana traffic to accepted industrial and medicinal channels, but he said that it did not follow that the levy was, therefore, invalid.

"It is beyond serious question that a tax does not cease to be valid merely because it regulates, discourages or even definitely deters the activities taxed," Mr. Clark asserted.

Furthermore, he said that the tax was not conditioned on the commission of a crime, and since "tax liability does not in effect rest on criminal conduct, the tax can be properly called a civil rather than a criminal sanction."

The Court sent the case back to Judge Barnes for "further proceedings in conformity" with today's decision.

House Group Votes Jail in Drug Cases

BY THE NEW YORK TIMES | JUNE 16, 1951

WASHINGTON, JUNE 15 — A bill calling for mandatory minimum jail sentences for violators of Federal narcotics laws was approved today by the House Ways and Means Committee.

The action was based on a sub-committee report that attributed a sharply rising rate of narcotics addiction and the booming illicit traffic largely to the leniency of courts in sentencing offenders.

The bill, sponsored by Representative Hale Boggs, Democrat of Louisiana, would require judges to impose sentences of at least two to five years for the first offense, five to ten years for the second and ten to twenty years for subsequent offenses. Maximum fines, to which violators would be also liable, would be set at $2,000, $5,000 and $2,000, respectively.

Suspended sentences and paroles still would be permitted upon the first conviction, but they would be barred for repeaters.

Under present law, persons who illegally import, conceal, transport, buy or sell opium, cocaine, heroin and similar narcotics are subject to a maximum penalty of ten years imprisonment and a $5,000 fine.

OPPOSITION TO FIXED SENTENCES

The same penalty is applicable to dealers in those narcotics and marijuana who fail to pay Federal "occupational" taxes. A maximum penalty of five years and $2,000 also is provided for selling marijuana without paying a Federal "transfer" tax. The penalties in the new bill would apply to all these offenses.

The Ways and Means Committee's vote on the bill was not announced, but it was reported that three and possibly four of the twenty-five members were opposed. Concern was voiced over the sharpness of the proposed penalties. There was also some opposition to the principle of compelling courts to impose specified sentences.

The subcommittee, headed by Representative Boggs, based its report on three days of hearings of its own and on a study of the transcript of hearings and recommendations of the Senate Crime Investigating Committee. Mandatory sentences of at least five years were recommended by the Senate committee while under the chairmanship of Senator Estes Kefauver, Democrat of Tennessee.

The subcommittee found that Federal judges in few areas had a record of having imposed severe sentences for narcotics violations. As an example of the effects of leniency, it cited testimony that narcotics peddlers living in Brooklyn no longer did business there because of prevailing severe sentences but had moved over into Manhattan, where the courts were held to be less severe.

The witness who testified to this was Harry J. Anslinger, Federal Commissioner of Narcotics, who was in charge of the Federal Narcotics Bureau's New York district in 1928, 1929 and 1940.

AVERAGE SENTENCE 23.1 MONTHS

"The judges at that time in Brooklyn," he said, "meted out strong, long sentences. Ten years was common. In Manhattan it was consistent with what it is at this time, and that condition maintains in New York at this time. They do not do business in Brooklyn. They may live in Brooklyn, but the deals are made in Manhattan, where prosecution would be in the event they were caught."

The average sentence throughout the country for a person convicted of violation of Federal narcotics and marijuana laws in the twelve months ended last June 30 was 23.1 months, the subcommittee reported. The percentage of persons receiving sentences of five years or more, it added, is less than for violation of counterfeiting and white slavery laws.

The subcommittee expressed concern over "an alarming increase in drug addiction among young people." In 1946, it reported, the United States Public Health Service at Lexington, Ky., had only three patients under 21 years of age, while in 1950 it had 766.

"The drug traffic," it added, "has also become a problem among personnel at our military establishments over the past several months. Dope peddlers have been arrested in and about several military camps and addiction has been detected among personnel of the armed services."

City Seeks to Kill Marijuana Weeds

BY THE NEW YORK TIMES | JUNE 20, 1951

A CAMPAIGN by the city to destroy marijuana growing in vacant lots in all five boroughs got under way yesterday at several points in Astoria and Long Island City, Queens.

Members of the Police Narcotics Bureau, under the command of Acting Lieut. Bernard Boylan, worked with teams from the Departments of Health and Sanitation. They began operations on a vacant lot at Thirty-seventh Avenue and Crescent Street, Long Island City, where large quantities of the narcotics-producing weed were found.

Under the supervision of Narcotics Bureau members, Health Department workers began spraying the plants, which grow to five feet in height and are distinguished by bright green, spear-shaped,

BROOKLYN PUBLIC LIBRARY, BROOKLYN COLLECTION

Chief Sanitation Inspector John E. Gleason directs three aides as they uproot a patch of marijuana.

tooth-edged leaves. They used 2,4-D, a plant hormone used to kill ragweed, which causes the plants to grow so fast that they soon wither and die. The teams then went to another lot at Thirty-first Street and Twenty-fourth Road, Astoria, where hundreds of the plants were found. There Sanitation workers uprooted the plants and prepared to weigh them. After their weights have been recorded with the Commissioner of Narcotics in Washington, they will be burned.

Altogether, six reported plots were investigated and four of them found to contain marijuana. Similar teams are expected to go to work immediately in the other boroughs, although Queens is believed to contain the greater part of the growth here.

Working with these specialized groups, under a recent departmental order, are all the police of the city. They are required, in the course of their normal duties, to report any suspicious growths to their commanding officers, who in turn report to the Narcotics Bureau.

Sgt. John F. Cottone, second in command of the bureau, said that most of the marijuana was growing wild just like any other weed.

He added, however, that there were some instances where ground was turned up around the plants indicating that someone was cultivating them.

In such cases, he said, the plant is not immediately destroyed. He could not say what action was taken in these circumstances but declared that "if we do not take prompt action, enough of it may be harvested to flood the local market."

John E. Gleason, Chief Inspector of the Sanitation Department, said that persons living in the areas of the vacant lots had been very helpful in giving information on the cultivated plants.

Neither man would estimate how many lots containing marijuana would be found. Inspector Gleason, however, said they might be working in Queens for a month or two.

"If we can get rid of half the stuff," he said, "we'll be doing a good job. But it would take a year or more if we checked on every report we've received, because lots of people think almost every weed they see is marijuana."

BROOKLYN PUBLIC LIBRARY, BROOKLYN COLLECTION

John E. Gleason inspects a marijuana plant taller than he with Sanitation District Superintendent Dennis Healy at right.

Sergeant Cottone said the reason for spraying some plants and uprooting others was experimental. Although marijuana plants have been destroyed in former years, he said this was the first concerted drive and it was not yet known which method of destruction was best.

The local product, he declared, has been "growing here since before I joined the bureau," which was nineteen years ago. He said it was probable that originally it was brought in to be cultivated by narcotics peddlers, but now it was mostly growing wild.

"But the situation is getting worse now," he said, "with the price of marijuana cigarettes going up from a dime to 50 cents and a dollar now. And the supply is steadily increasing. The plant's seeds resemble bird seed and birds pick them up and drop them in other spots. If we don't destroy them now, there will be even more of them next year."

CHAPTER 2

1960s–70s: From the Village to Vietnam, Embracing Pot

In the 1960s, the narrative around cannabis use shifted in the United States. The counterculture of the hippies and beatniks embraced cannabis and LSD. Further, its prevalence among students and U.S. soldiers in Vietnam contributed to a counternarrative to the association of "stoners" with heroin addicts and users of other narcotics. Medical studies began to focus on its therapeutic uses, while debunking popular myths that exaggerated the consequences of its use.

Narcotics a Growing Problem of Affluent Youth

BY MARTIN ARNOLD | JAN. 4, 1965

"IT'S THE BIG THING, the hip thing to do. A friend of mine, we were talking one day and the subject of marijuana kept coming up. It ended up we got together and I turned on for the first time."

The speaker, David, a tall 19-year-old student at the Juilliard School of Music, is not a narcotics addict, but he is representative of the increasing number of young people from the substantial, the sophisticated and the educated families of the city and its suburbs who are using marijuana, barbiturates and addictive narcotics.

This affluent narcotics user, who starts as a teenager with marijuana or "goof balls" (barbiturates) and later becomes "hooked" on heroin, has complicated even further what the Police Department says has become its No. 1 problem — the use of and traffic in narcotics.

He does it not to flee the misery of the slums but because he wants kicks, because experimenting with narcotics is "in," is "hip," is considered even more challenging than the sex and liquor parties of a generation ago.

The seriousness of the problem was underlined on Saturday by Governor Rockefeller, who called for massive state and Federal programs to combat narcotics addiction in the state.

Unofficially, the police estimate that about 35 per cent of the marijuana smokers like David will eventually become addicted to narcotics. Of the other 65 per cent, some will seek, and be helped by, psychotherapy; some will pull out of the habit on their own, dismiss it as a youthful phase; and many will settle into a rootless, goalless existence in which marijuana will be a vague but basic element, like changing partners, lodgings and jobs.

The use of marijuana and other narcotics, which began spreading years ago from the city's slum areas, has during the last five years increased considerably in Greenwich Village, the new Bohemia of the Lower East Side, the neighborhoods surrounding the city's universities, and the suburbs, according to the police.

Because the world of the drug user is a subterranean one, there are no accurate statistics available on the number of people using narcotics. Most of the figures are based on observations and inferences by the police and by medical and social agencies.

The estimates of the number of addicts in the city, those who are hooked on heroin (horse) or other narcotics, range from an avowedly conservative 23,000 persons to a possibly exaggerated 100,000 persons. These figures do not include the marijuana users.

COMPARED TO DRINKING

There is no estimate of the number of Davids in the city, or the number of girls like Betty, a recent honor graduate from Hunter College. She tosses back her long brown hair, calls smoking marijuana (pot) "a gas" and says she started the same way others start drinking socially. She rationalizes her habit this way:

> *I have control with pot. If I drink I might go to a party and go home and go to bed with someone. It's happened. But never with pot.*

David has been smoking marijuana since he was a high school senior. He "turns on" once or twice a week, buying his marijuana with the $20-a-week allowance his mother gives him on Tuesdays.

Is marijuana a habit for David?

David says it isn't, but he also says, "I sort of got used to using it. After a time it became an integral part of what I do." He insists, though, it is not necessary for him.

POSSESSION IS ILLEGAL

Marijuana has not been proved to be medically harmful or addictive. But it can become as habit-forming as cigarettes, and its possession is illegal because it has proved to be a first step, in many cases, to heroin and other narcotics.

Marijuana is one of the three general classifications of narcotics covered by the State Health and Penal Laws and by the City Police Department Narcotics Bureau. The others are the cocaines, which are nonaddictive, and the opiates, such as heroin and opium, which are addictive.

But the marijuana user tends to slip into a milieu in which drugs and the kicks they supply become the focal point of his social activity. The smoker is casual about — indeed proud of — the fact that some of his friends have gone beyond marijuana to heroin.

And because the continual smoker is often deeply disturbed emotionally — using marijuana to release his tensions and brighten his world —

he often comes to the psychological crossroads where he seeks help or flees further from reality with the addictive drugs, such as heroin.

ADDICTION LEADS TO CRIME

The police files are filled with cases of young women from well-to-do families who have turned to prostitution and well-educated young men and women who commit crimes against person and property as their addiction requires more and more money.

Dr. Graham B. Blaine Jr., psychiatrist to the Harvard and Radcliffe Health Service, describes the social phenomenon of the affluent addict as an "unconscious" hunt for "danger — playing with fire."

"It springs from affluence," Dr. Blaine says. "We give young people a lot. When a young man can raise his finger and mama gives him a Jaguar, things are too easy. He has never been tested in real danger.

"Never having been tested, they are distasteful of themselves and are trying to alter with drugs their personalities. They are trying to change an unconscious weltschmerz — world of pain — which is more than apathy, which is neutral. They have a lack of hope with the world at large and themselves in it."

MOTIVATIONS ASSAYED

Dr. Blaine says marijuana and cocaine users often have the psychological "tendency and motivation to go on to heroin if given the opportunity, and they can usually get heroin from the same suppliers who sell marijuana."

And because most of these people who become addicts do so in their late 20's and early 30's, the inference is that they were usually on marijuana or some nonaddictive drug for a long time before they yielded to the desire for the greater sensation of heroin.

Marijuana is easily purchased in most sections of the city. Heroin, while harder to get, is also readily available, except when there is a shortage or "panic."

Because there was a slowdown in the manufacture of heroin overseas — and to a lesser extent because of a police crackdown here — there was such a panic in October and November, but it has now eased off.

SOCIETY MORE PERMISSIVE

So far as the individual is concerned the marijuana smoker and the narcotics addict are more a medical than a police problem; and thus, many experts believe, society in attempting to deal with the problem of addiction perhaps runs into a contradiction.

It is that while many smokers and addicts indulge first as an act of rebellion, they also do so with the mental cushion that society is now more understanding and permissive about the use of drugs. (In Britain, for example, addicts are often legally maintained on their addiction.)

Marijuana, among the better educated, has a mystique all its own. It and heroin and other drugs also are the subject of a number of myths, the fundamental ones being that there is a cure for addiction and that marijuana cannot become a harmful habit.

Marijuana is classified by the experts as an excitant, although with continual use it can become a depressant. For some persons, it is always a depressant.

EFFECTS DESCRIBED

It distorts time and space, and the user often has a slight floating sensation. At the same time, he feels that he is functioning in slow motion.

Marijuana generally releases inhibition and makes one susceptible to suggestion. Some people say it is a sex stimulant, but others find it has the opposite effect, deadening all sexual desire.

Most young people who smoke marijuana start at a party. Either they have gone to the party because they have heard that marijuana would be smoked and wanted to try it, or they have been dared to smoke it once they were there; or they did not want to feel left out.

In case after case, among an increasing range of people, an observer found that the smoking of marijuana had become a status symbol. The young adults who smoked it considered themselves pace-setters and disdained people who would not try it.

At some parties it was done casually. Several people would light up — either a cigarette or a pipe — and then hand it around. The conversation for most part was about the sensations. Those who declined, more often girls than men, were considered "square," out of things.

'A BUILT-IN STEREO'

Habitual users nearly always contend that marijuana intensifies feelings, that it sharpens perceptions. Betty, the young Hunter College graduate, says: "With pot you hear all the music, all the instruments. It's like a built-in stereo."

She is 21 years old, and lives in a two-room apartment in Greenwich Village with an artist who is nearly 20 years older. Betty moved to the "Village" shortly before she graduated from college last June.

Her family comes from the Bronx and her father recently retired from a $15,000-a-year job and moved with her mother to Florida. She doesn't like her older sister, because she lives in a hotel for women, which has a curfew for residents.

"When I started with pot I never thought about it. I just trusted the person I was with," Betty said. "The first time I turned on, the whole apartment went blue and purple. What a gas!"

Betty was seated on one of the two rumpled beds in the apartment, for which she pays $56 a month. The ash trays overflowed onto the desk and the cheap wooden end tables. She was wearing a white sweater turned gray, which matched her slacks. Michael, the artist, was leaning against the wall drinking a beer, and he said:

> *If you are walking down the street you see everything around you. You see all you normally see but you now are acutely aware. With liquor you lose a great deal. You don't really experience what's going on around you.*

AFRAID OF 'NEXT STEP'

Michael is the third man Betty has been living with in the "Village," and she has had brief affairs in between. She doesn't smoke regularly, she says, but "only when it's around."

"I don't want to take the next step, heroin," she says. "Say I'm a bit scary about that.

"But I'd like to have enough money not to go to work and stay turned on for a month. The way it is now you know you are staying turned on for two hours and then coming down again. That's it."

Betty's introduction to narcotics is somewhat typical. In spite of stories to the contrary, pushers almost never haunt schoolyards and recreation areas in an attempt to find new customers. Most users say they began because a friend urged them.

SOLD IN $5 BAGS

The usual unit of marijuana purchase is the nickel ($5) bag, which contains enough for about 12 cigarettes. Dime ($10) and quarter ($25) bags are also sold. The contents are usually smoked, in rolled cigarettes or pipes, but can be chewed or put into food and drink.

Betty, when she has time, writes short stories, but has never sold any. She and Michael listen to music, attend the opera and cruise the bars of the East Village with friends.

They buy a $5 bag of marijuana from a friend, who in turn gets it from another friend, who is a pusher.

"I meet my friend, say in a coffeehouse or bar, and he'll shove a pack of cigarettes across the table, only there wouldn't be cigarettes in it — it's stuffed with pot," she says.

There are in Greenwich Village, which is becoming the main area for marijuana suppliers outside the slums, several coffeehouses frequented by marijuana users mostly, but also by heroin addicts.

IT IS EASILY AVAILABLE

In a half dozen bars on the Lower East Side, crude and dirty where

Villagers and slummers mingle, marijuana and other drugs are sold.

The availability is such that on a recent visit to the "Village" an observer, who had never seen marijuana before, was able to purchase a $5 bag from strangers within two hours. It came in an envelope marked Graduate School of Journalism, Columbia University.

One of the problems in suppressing marijuana is that it is a weed that will grow almost anywhere with little care.

A marijuana cigarette is called a joint by a user. The butts are called "roaches," and are saved to be smoked after the effect has nearly worn off; and the user wants to get back a slight glow.

The music student, David, first started on marijuana when he was a senior in the High School of Music and Art. "A kid starts the same way he starts cigarettes," David said. "He whips behind the shed or door and whips out a butt and starts choking with it at first, but keeps it up — keeping up with the Joneses sort of thing.

"There comes a point where I can channel my thoughts more clearly. I can separate that which is really bothering me from the trivial. When I'm really bugged I smoke heavily, and there are days when I'm completely stoned."

BOY EXPLAINS PRESSURES

David lives with his parents, both successful classical musicians. One or both are often away from home.

"Maybe I feel pressure because I'm not yet successful. My mother is a little high-strung and I'm high-strung. My throat gets scratchy, and I turn on."

He speaks in contradictions.

First he may say: "In two years on pot I've had enough time to get a preliminary judgment of myself. I really don't foresee becoming too dependent on it. That's why I know I'll never get hooked on heroin."

But a minute later he will say: "I don't smoke it any more often because I've become quite afraid that I'll soon need even far more. I can go weeks and months without pot, but I don't expect to because I'm in control, so why worry?"

A smoker rarely indulges alone. He almost always smokes in social situations, often at so-called "pot parties." He does not hoard his marijuana but shares it. It is this way with David, who smokes marijuana often during sessions with fellow students.

The same is most often true of those who begin their drug experiments with cough medicine high in codeine, the barbiturates and Benzedrine, referred to as pep pills and bennies. These have become particularly popular at teen-age suburban narcotic parties in private homes and parked automobiles on secluded streets.

LEGISLATION IS URGED

In fact, so smart has the smoking of marijuana become that an organization known as Lemar has been founded in San Francisco to fight the legal restrictions against it. Allen Ginsberg, the poet, is a leading New York member of Lemar, which stands for "Legalize Marijuana."

But the sociability factor is not true of the "junkie" who is on heroin. Heroin, and the pursuit of it, becomes the junkie's whole life. He will more than hoard; if forced, he will kill for it.

The use of heroin becomes an addiction. The addict is physiologically and psychologically hooked on heroin and other drugs such as opium. A "main-liner" — an addict who injects heroin directly into the bloodstream — for example, will eventually reach the point that the drug no longer provides him with euphoria and grandiose dreams.

Rather, he needs it simply to function. That is why some addicts will voluntarily enter hospitals, not to be cured, but to bring their tolerance of heroin back to a point where they get their kicks and can afford the habit.

A DOWNWARD TRAIL

Ann, 25, is a secretary-book-keeper with two years of college. She came to New York five years ago from the Middle West, where her father was a contractor. She has a brother and two sisters, all of whom still live in the Middle West. She went from marijuana to heroin this way:

> *I went out to a party with a boy friend I had started living with. He was an addict. I got drunk and when I woke up at home, he was pulling the needle out of my arm, and I got very high. I didn't like it or dislike it, but the next day I got sick and he gave me another shot.*
>
> *I knew it was bad, but I liked it very much because I liked getting high without alcohol. I found at first when I was high I could do things I couldn't when I was straight. Like walk into a room without feeling everybody was watching me.*

In the course of her addiction, she has lived with several men, has married addicts twice and has had two children, has stolen money and property, cashed bad checks and turned to prostitution, for which she was arrested once. When she got to the point that she had to buy about $35 worth a day, she entered the hospital to withdraw — cleanse her body of heroin.

Psychologically, however, she will still be hooked.

"I know I can cure myself if I can get anything I want," she says. "A nice home and a good job. But the people I know — even my family — I don't think they will take me back. So I'll try. But you know the only ones who will take me back are the junkies and pushers and pimps."

HOOKED BY A FRIEND

There is Joan, 22, whose father owns a small manufacturing plant in Westchester and whose mother teaches school "just for something to do." She is an only child, who started on marijuana at the age of 16 and shortly thereafter, "looking for even greater kicks," was hooked on heroin by a boy friend.

Joan is an example of what Dr. Felicia Oliver-Smith, senior public health physician of the city Health Department's narcotics division, calls the "peer-oriented."

"Many of these kids have tremendous emotional problems," Dr. Oliver-Smith says. "They don't respect their parents. Authority figures now have much less authority than before. It's peer acceptance that is important to them."

At her parents' behest, Joan has been in and out of hospitals six times. She seldom goes to Westchester, but when she does she steals the silverware, her mother's jewelry and everything else that is easily transportable to sell to maintain her addiction.

She has had an out-of-wedlock child, who had been placed for adoption. After Joan is home for several days her parents become as desperate as she does; her father, at times accompanied by her mother, will drive her to the city and drop her off on a street corner, usually near Chinatown, where, they know, she will solicit for prostitution. She has tried, feebly, to get rid of her addiction, but asks:

> *Why bother? Who would have me? After what I've been, would you marry me?*

OTHER DRUGS IN USE

The connection between marijuana and heroin is often as straight as a railroad track. But in recent years a number of stopovers have become popular. They are the so-called mind-expanding drugs (psilocybin, mescaline, peyote, ground morning-glory seeds and LSD); the opiates and synthetics (codeine, Dilaudid, paregoric, Demerol and Methadone); and the addicting but nonnarcotic barbiturates (Seconal, Nembutal and the sleeping pills or goof balls).

The mind-expanding drugs are hallucinogens, as are the pep pills and the bennies. Most other drugs, like heroin, produce euphoria, stupor, intoxication, slovenliness and lethargy. Popular now is amyl nitrate, which comes in phials and is used to treat artery-disease patients.

One sniff and the user has an hallucination that lasts perhaps 30 seconds.

All of these, but particularly heroin, present an unusual problem for the police in a city like New York, which is believed to have at least one-half of the addicts in the country. To sell heroin, marijuana or other narcotics is a felony, punishable by a possible, but rarely pronounced, 15-year prison sentence. To possess these narcotics can be a felony or a misdemeanor, depending on how much one has.

200 IN NARCOTICS BUREAU

The Police Narcotics Bureau is the largest such unit operating in a single place in the world. It has 200 men and women headed by Inspector Ira Bluth, an articulate City College graduate, who has been a policeman since 1940.

Police work in narcotics is subtle and difficult. There is seldom a beginning to a case, except as it is developed by the bureau itself. Unlike a robbery, for example, the victim in the narcotics case — the addict — is never a complainant.

The informant is nearly always a user who has been arrested and who informs rather than go to jail.

Inspector Bluth sums up the narcotic problem this way:

> *One woman, whose son is an addict, came in recently and told me that she hopes there will be a day when "I come home from work and am notified that my son is dead. Tell me he's dead. I have a daughter. She's still O.K., but I'm afraid for her. Tell me he's dead."*

Four G.I.'s Are Accused of Possessing Narcotics, 20 Under Inquiry

BY R. W. APPLE JR. | JAN. 27, 1966

ANKHS, SOUTH VIETNAM, JAN. 26 — Four soldiers of the United States First Cavalry Division (Airmobile) have been charged with illegally possessing narcotics, and 20 are under investigation.

Lieut. Col. H. W. Uhland of Yorktown Heights, N. Y., the division provost marshal, said in an interview that he was conducting "an intensive investigation" of narcotics in this village, which lies just outside the First Cavalry compound, 260 miles northeast of Saigon.

No members of the First Cavalry have been permitted to go into the village since Jan. 20. The restriction was imposed for security reasons during the Lunar New Year holiday but has been kept in force since because of the traffic in narcotics and several other problems.

Although there are conflicting reports, it appears that most if not all of the servicemen who are under investigation are suspected of having used marijuana.

Some opium is also known to have been offered for sale, but responsible sources said there had been no cases of addiction here.

Marijuana, a nonaddictive drug, is usually not considered a narcotic in civilian medical practice; opium causes addiction.

The arrests are one element in a situation that has worried senior officers here.

"The village is explosive," one of them said, "and getting worse."

Until the 16,000 men of the First Cavalry began arriving Sept. 12, Ankhe was a sleepy hamlet nestled in the flatlands between two ranges of mountains athwart Highway 19.

Now it is an Oriental boom town, Virginia City in the rice paddles.

Shacks made of beer cans provide beer, bar girls and dolls and other Vietnamese gewgaws.

Several months ago, the district officer, Tran Duoc Vu, told American officers he would limit the number of bars to 45 and the number of bar girls to 350. There are now 61 bars and 511 bar girls.

Forced to operate with a limited police force and confronted by greedy merchants, many with political and military connections, Mr. Vu has been powerless to supervise either the bar girls or what is sold in the bars.

Lieut. Col. Monroe Kirkpatrick, the division's assistant civic affairs officer, said that United States and Vietnamese Government authorities hoped to open next month a center near Ankhe containing 48 bars with eight girls each. All the other bars in the village would be closed.

"The center will have a wire fence around it," Colonel Kirkpatrick, a good-humored man from Arkansas, explained. "It will have only one entrance. It should be easy for the local police to keep track of things there.

The bar girls, many of whom are prostitutes, will be examined regularly by South Vietnamese medical teams with the assistance of American doctors. The Americans recognize that acceptance of quasi-official prostitution here will not be popular in the United States, but they consider it the only practical alternative to rampant venereal disease.

According to some in the First Cavalry, it has been possible recently to buy enough marijuana to make 20 cigarettes for the equivalent of $5, and to have an opium derivative added to a beer for 45 cents.

Some reports indicate that opium pipes are available.

The situation came to the attention of the division when a military policeman found a soldier in a bar early this month with a fistful of crumpled greenish-brown marijuana leaves. After he was questioned, several of his friends were also charged with possessing narcotics.

Military policemen in subsequent raids seized 2 to 10 pounds of opium and marijuana at various places in the village.

NAMES KEPT SECRET

The provost marshal said the soldiers charged with illegal possession had been "extremely cooperative" and had been continued in their duty assignments. Their names have not been made public.

If brought to trial and found guilty by a court-martial, any of the suspects could be sentenced to five years in prison — a fact noted in a recent issue of the division's daily bulletin.

The division surgeon, Lieut. Col. James E. McCary of Fort Worth, Tex., who first identified the narcotics that were seized, said he viewed the use of narcotics as "extremely serious" but nevertheless as an "entirely understandable" development.

"If you get 12,000 or 16,000 boys together," he said, "some of them will act like jerks. They think they aren't men until they get V.D. and smoke pot and there's nothing you can do to stop them."

Drugs a Growing Campus Problem

BY JOHN CORRY | MARCH 21, 1966

HIS NAME was Steve, he wore a beard, and he lived with a blonde who had a voice like Lauren Bacall's. He was pleasant and candid (nice old ladies would say that he was such a sweet young man) and he regularly turned on with marijuana or blew his mind with LSD.

"Fifty per cent," he was saying, "maybe 50 per cent of the kids at school use drugs." His school was San Francisco State College, and across the Bay at the Berkeley campus of the University of California a criminologist said that perhaps 40 per cent of the students there used drugs from time to time.

There is a numbers game involved in this; actually, no one knows, even approximately, how many students take drugs. But everyone agrees that the number is rising, that it has been for several years, and that no one is quite sure what to do about it.

Visits to a half-dozen campuses show that "hard" narcotics, for instance heroin, are not used and that marijuana and LSD are the drugs most commonly resorted to. Who uses them? Graduate students mostly, but more often than not the pattern among undergraduates is this:

The drug takers are majoring in the humanities or social sciences, with more in English than any other subject. There are fewer consistent users in the sciences or in the professional schools.

Proportionately, a great many seem to show up in anthropology. A professor at Berkeley recalls that when a visiting lecturer spoke to the anthropology majors about the Indians of the American Southwest "it damn near turned into a recipe-swapping session for peyote and the magic mushrooms."

They are not churchgoers, which may seem obvious. But they are not dedicated Communists, either. ("Communism shrinks your head," a marijuana smoker at the University of Chicago said.)

Disciplined ideologies do not attract them and disciplined campus ideologists, who tend to be joyless, anyway, consider them frivolous.

They are vaguely leftist, disenchanted with American policies in Vietnam, agitated because there are Negro ghettos and bored with conventional politics. They do not join the Peace Corps, which, a Student at Penn State said, "is for Boy Scouts."

Their fathers, more often than not, are professional men or white collar executives. They are not deprived. A California psychiatrist says that the children of television writers in Hollywood use drugs more than any other group.

Students who smoke marijuana regularly, but not often and not much, are different than heavy, consistent users. For one thing, the first group — call them weekend users — is more self-conscious about drugs and is periodically swept by rumors, especially about the police.

The other day in Boulder, Colo., home of the University of Colorado, a student and his girl, both weekend marijuana smokers, sat and snuffed out cigarette butts in their coffee cups and spoke about what they called "the situation."

They said there was a $50,000 cache of LSD on the campus, that four professors were under surveillance, that the town was swarming with narcotics agents, and that a police raid was imminent.

A SOURCE OF RUMORS

Another student, a user who had just casually displayed a vial of LSD capsules, made a face and said he had heard in the afternoon that it was $30,000 worth of LSD, that he wondered where the narcotics agents were hiding, that police raids were always imminent, and why should anyone be concerned with what four professors did.

This is the way it is across the country, and this is why it is difficult to distinguish fact from fancy about the drug takers; they are very big with rumors.

The chief psychiatrist at the Berkeley campus of the University of California says that up to 20 per cent of the students there may be smoking marijuana. There are 27,000 students on the campus and marijuana, he says, is "just part of the scene."

Furthermore, he guesses that at any big-city university or sophisticated, small liberal arts college, 10 per cent of the students will experiment with LSD or marijuana. Few who are intimately connected with students challenge the figures.

However, a few blocks away a police inspector says there are no more than 200 students at Berkeley who turn on regularly. There were 198 narcotics arrests last year, he says, and only 10 of them involved students. He adds that the department uses civilian undercover agents who are paid $50 a week and that not much gets by them.

Furthermore, the inspector is convinced that there are no drugs at all in Berkeley High School.

At Pepe's Pizza ("famous among beatniks," a policeman says), a homely girl in a granny dress and a boy with matted hair identify themselves as students at Berkeley High School and say, yes, lots of high-school students smoke marijuana. They both do, they say, and "the fuzz," the police, even with their undercover agents, simply aren't smart enough to catch them.

While drugs can, and often do, leap from the underworld to the campus there is sometimes an unmistakably adolescent air about their consumption. At Penn State the pot smokers sit in the Hub, which is the student union, and use a wholly unnecessary slang and system of code names to befuddle the police.

(One of their listeners has been an imaginative and conscientious police sergeant named John Snedden; nine students were arrested last month.)

In Boulder, a night club called The Sink is fabulously wicked. It is a block from the university and it is dark and depraved. The marijuana smokers slink in and out, but without lighting up inside, which would be considered gauche. The other night a man asked for a bourbon and water there and was told that The Sink serves only 3.2 beer, and that you must be 21 for it.

For the most part, the drugs are classified as amphetamines, barbituates or hallucinogens, and of these the hallucinogens are the most prominent.

About 80 hallucinogens have been identified in the Western world and they are sometimes referred to as psychedelic, which means mind manifesting, or as consciousness expanding. Marijuana, the most common, is classed by Federal law with heroin and other narcotics, but, nevertheless, it is a true hallucinogen.

Marijuana is made from the dry, flowery tops of the female Indian hemp plant, called cannabis sativa by botanists. It is smoked in pipes or in cigarettes, which on campus are called joints or sticks, never reefers. It grows like crabgrass in all parts of the country, but users prefer the Mexican variety.

Sticks cost from 50 cents to $1.50 apiece, with the higher prices predominating away from New York or California, the main distribution points. The more sophisticated users, however, buy it by the ounce, which costs from $15 to $25 and in the Western states is called a can or a lid. It provides about 30 cigarettes.

Marijuana has names like weed, grass, tea, Mary Jane and gage, but usually it is called pot. Student pot parties, those wild abandoned orgies in which no man's daughter is safe, seem to exist more in fancy than in fact.

THE DRINK IS WINE

Most pot is smoked at the end of conventional parties by a few hangers-on or else in small groups, where it is associated with feelings of conviviality or warmth. Moreover, there is some indication that heavy users of marijuana have less interest in sex than do non-users. They also seem to have less interest in alcohol; their drink is wine.

None of which is to say that marijuana cannot be dangerous. A significant number of marijuana smokers will go on to heroin, the Bureau of Narcotics says. "Potsville," the narcotics agents say, "leads to the mainline."

Other common hallucinogens are mescaline, which is a chemical taken from the tops, or buttons, of the peyote cactus; psilocybin, which is synthesized from a variety of Mexican mushrooms, and LSD-25, a synthetic made from lysergic acid diethylamide. Students call it acid.

LSD is the most potent hallucinogen. Students tell of LSD ingressions (trips, they call them) and of profound, sometimes terrifying, experiences. "It is not the flashing lights and visual distortions," a student in San Francisco says, "It is the psychedelic soul-searching."

The LSD users speak of dissolving the ego, meeting the naked self, finding a truly religious experience and being so terribly honest with themselves that they know that all about them is sham. They call LSD things like a psychic energizer and say that it offers them a creative release. But essentially, they say, a trip is an incommunicable experience.

The Food and Drug Administration, which regulates and polices LSD, just calls it the country's fastest growing drug problem. It has horror stories to support this, and so do most university clinics.

An 18-year-old at Berkeley took LSD and tried to jump off a bridge. After his experiment a student at the University of Colorado developed a compulsion to flick imaginary bugs from his body. Months after her trip a girl in San Francisco was hospitalized with a full-blown psychosis; her doctors attributed it to LSD.

A capsule containing 200 to 600 micrograms of LSD will sell from $1 to $10, with an average price around $5. Virtually any competent chemist can make it for the illicit market, and apparently many do. One estimate is that a thousand times as much LSD is taken illegally as in authorized experimentation.

The amphetamines, known as pep pills, stimulate the central nervous system. They hide fatigue and offer instant euphoria, exhilaration and a sense of great acuteness. They can be habit forming, just as cigarettes can be, but they are not addictive.

ADDICTION IS POSSIBLE

Barbiturates, in turn, calm the central nervous system, and they can be addictive. That is, the user can develop a tolerance to the drug so that the same amount produces progressively less effect; he must continue to take it to prevent withdrawal symptoms, and he may turn to it during emotional stress.

Of all the drugs found on campuses, barbiturates are the only ones that produce these characteristics of addiction. When properly prescribed and used they have no harmful effect. But if taken wantonly they leave the user bewildered, without a sense of time and unable to reason logically. An overdose can depress respiratory control until breathing is stopped.

Besides these, there are on college campuses and in high schools an enormous variety of patent medicines, condiments, household items and garden weeds that are used to produce illusion, oblivion or simple stupefaction.

They include cough medicines, airplane glue, diet aids, cleaning fluids, pepper, nutmeg, asthma therapeutics, relaxing drugs and morning-glory seeds. They are nearly ubiquitous, but they are probably found more in high schools than in colleges.

As a rule of thumb, the Bureau of Narcotics says, when a drug more sophisticated than cough medicine or morning-glory seeds is found on a rural campus there is probably a student from New York or California involved. He is the one with a line into the big-city distributor or the vast, informal and effective college underground.

At smaller schools, most drug takers, especially the heavier users, know one another. In addition, they know other students on other campuses. There is a good deal of driving back and forth, a great many telephone calls, a lot of letters. This is the basis of the college underground.

Last month a student from Bradley University in Peoria, Ill., and a student from Sarah Lawrence College in Bronxville, N. Y., who was the daughter of a Hollywood television producer, were arrested in Chicago after about $2,500 worth of marijuana had been found in their luggage.

Typically, the college underground does not deal in such quantities. In Berkeley, for instance, on any given day there are from 1,500 to 2,500 semiretired students and beatnik types living near the campus. They are restless and ambulatory, and it is not particularly difficult for one to cross into Mexico, buy a kilogram of marijuana for $20 and sell it in Berkeley for $200.

It might be sold to one particular sophomore, who will immediately divide it and distribute it to some of the eight students who work for him. The sophomore, incidentally, will not hold the marijuana very long himself. He is far too cautious.

OTHER TYPES SHOW UP

Other types also show up on campus as distributors. Marijuana at the University of Chicago is sometimes sold by sophisticated, well dressed Negroes in their mid-twenties who pass themselves off as students or former students.

Their source of supply is the Old Town section, about 20 blocks from the Loop, which not long ago was full of seedy bars and sleeping vagrants and is now a sort of clean Greenwich Village, touched by both the giddy and the garish.

No matter what else is said about drugs the final question is why do students take them. Why do they risk convictions for a felony and move so often into the world of sour apartments where they must work hard to hide their habit from the squares, which is how they refer, quite dispassionately, to nonusers?

Why do they increasingly drop out of school and join the LSD cult, there to contemplate nature, induce periodic insanity and pursue a philosophy that is a curious mélange of Zen, Aldous Huxley, existentialism and leftover Orientalism?

Dr. John D. Walmer, director of the mental health clinic at Penn State, suggests that "for people who are chronically unhappy drugs bring some relief from a world without purpose."

George H. Gaffney, deputy commissioner of narcotics, says students take drugs because "of the growing disrespect for authority, because some professors just don't care to set any kind of moral influence and because of the growing beatnik influence.

Dr. Harvey Powleson, director of the psychiatric clinic at the Berkeley campus of the University of California, notes "a connection toward mystical movements in general." He tends to see users as dropouts from the Great Society.

Students themselves are not particularly articulate about why they take drugs. For kicks, they say, or because they are bored, or because drugs are easy to get, or because drugs offer them deep personal insights, or because they do not believe anything anyone has ever told them about drugs and they want to find out for themselves (a slogan of the Free Speech Movement at Berkeley was "Don't talk to anyone over 30"), or because they want to express distaste for split-level society, or because they are mixed up emotionally, or because they are products of a permissive age and what-can-you-expect from-children-who-had-charge-accounts-and-automobiles-at-16?

They do not talk about living in a world they never made, which they would consider trite, but sometimes this is what they mean, and when they imply it they are self-conscious and sometimes a little mawkish. For drugs, in a sense, are the ultimate, as well as the hippest, student protest. They offer an illicit pleasure that is almost entirely without sanction in the adult world and they open an immense gap between parent and child.

A boy at San Francisco State may have spoken for his generation when he said he smoked marijuana and used LSD "because there is just no reason not to." He was absolutely sure that this was so.

Police Look On as Hippies Stage a Park Smoke-In

BY STEPHEN A. O. GOLDEN | JULY 31, 1967

THE SWEET, HEAVY SMELL that indicates burning marijuana drifted over Tompkins Square Park on the Lower East Side yesterday evening. The hippies were having a "smoke-in," and seven policemen were standing by doing nothing about it.

About 200 young people gathered between two gnarled trees and smoked marijuana for over three hours. No arrests were made, though possession or smoking of marijuana is either a misdemeanor or a felony, depending on the quantity involved.

One officer said an arrest would "cause more trouble than it was worth."

A group known as Provo — from provocateur — which is described as being an organization of "subversive dope fiends" — sponsored the event.

AUDIENCE JOINS IN

The smoke-in began at about 7:15 P.M., when a band called the Pteradactyls began playing electric guitars. They called for the audience to come on stage and play the drums, and five Puerto Ricans heeded the call.

"That's the best part of this," one grass-smoking hippie said. "The hippies and the Puerto Ricans have one thing in common — grass. From that, a great relationship is being built up."

Marijuana is called grass, as well as pot, tea and Mary Jane.

Provo had a smoke-in last Sunday and the Sunday before. Each started with the smoking of banana peels (a relatively new hippie craze), but marijuana was smoked each time before the evening was out.

This time, though, the grass was handed out at once. As soon as the music started, the joints — as marijuana cigarettes are called —

LARRY MORRIS/THE NEW YORK TIMES

A policeman turns down offer to smoke a "joint" of marijuana.

were lit. At least seven policemen, including a captain, were standing by.

"It probably isn't pot," said Patrolman John Halbig. "I don't know if you know how to smoke pot, but you can't smoke it in the open air. It's probably banana anyway."

As he was talking, a hippie lit a joint and smoked peacefully, listening to the patrolman.

At one point, two boys walked into the crowd with two large brown paper bags full of joints. They threw the marijuana up in the air, and the crowd of 200 grabbed and scrambled for the falling cigarettes.

OVATION FOR POLICE

A minute later, two policemen walked into the crowd to "see what those cigarettes were." Five people opened a circle in the crowd and offered five burning objects to the policemen. Two were filter cigarettes, but three looked very much like marijuana.

One of the policemen waved his hand, and both walked out of the group. They were given an ovation by the smokers.

As the people stood in small circles passing joints from hand to hand, they would reach across and shake hands. "I'm Roger," one would say, trying to hold his breath so none of the smoke would escape prematurely.

"I'm Juan, George" ... "Steve" ... "Judy" ... "Pedro."

"We need more girls," one hippie yelled.

"No, man. We need more grass," said a Puerto Rican.

"Let's help the cops," one hippie said. "We'll put up a sign that says: 'Don't walk on the grass — smoke it.' "

Marijuana Held a Public Hazard

BY ROBERT R. REINHOLD | SEPT. 26, 1967

BOSTON, SEPT 25 — A New York psychiatrist described marijuana today as a "harmful and dangerous substance" that should be prohibited as a "hazard to public health."

"With every use of this substance," he said, "there will be a price to pay in abuse."

The psychiatrist Dr. Henry Brill is director of Pilgrim State Hospital on Long Island and a consultant on drug use to state and Federal agencies.

He was testifying in Suffolk County Superior Court as a hearing to test the constitutionality of the Massachusetts marijuana laws entered its second week.

"It is my opinion," stated Dr. Brill, "that the unrestricted use of marijuana type substances produces a significant amount of vagabondage, dependency and psychiatric disability. It tends to remove a significant number of producing people from society and make them dependent."

While marijuana smokers normally experience euphoria and great self-satisfaction, said Dr. Brill, there sometimes occur other, less pleasurable reactions.

He cited the following in calm professional tones:

- Severe bouts of anxiety.

- Psychiatric disorders, such as sudden psychotic changes in persons using large doses for a long time.

- Possible clouding of memory.

- Loss of desire "to do."

'PSYCHIC DEPENDENCE'

Users do not become physically dependent on marijuana, said Dr. Brill, but it does frequently result in "psychic dependence," which he defined as a compulsive drive to take the drug even when it damages the individual and society around him.

This type of dependence is even more difficult to treat than physical dependence because it "tends to promote relapse even throughout the entire life of the individual," while physical dependence can be broken in a few days, he said.

Dr. Brill was called by the prosecutor, James D. St Clair, as a state witness in the case of two Philadelphia men, Ivan Weiss and Joseph D. Leif, both 25, accused of possessing marijuana and possession with intent to sell.

The case has attracted national interest because the defense is attempting to set aside the Massachusetts marijuana laws, which are typical of those in many states.

The defense lawyer, Joseph S. Oteri, contends that marijuana should not be classified with heroin as a dangerous drug and that therefore, the penalties for marijuana possession under Massachusetts law are unconstitutionally harsh.

Early in the day a sociologist and a pharmaceutical chemist testified for the defense.

The sociologist, Bruce Jackson of the State University of New York at Buffalo, described the results of a three-year study of middle-class adult marijuana-users in New York City, Boston and Austin, Tex.

He said he had found no evidence that marijuana led to the use of more powerful drugs, to automobile accidents, sexual promiscuity, violent behavior or criminal activity.

The pharmaceutical chemist, Dr. Sanford J. Feinglass, who is a staff assistant for drug abuse for the Marin County school system in California, said that marijuana had potential therapeutic value in medicine.

The Drug Scene: Many Students Now Regard Marijuana as a Part of Growing Up

BY JOHN KIFNER | JAN. 11, 1968

AMHERST, MASS., is a New England college town, dominated by a sweeping tree-shaded green, flanked on the south by a small business section, and on the north by comfortable fraternity houses and the pretty campus of Amherst College.

It looks like the setting for one of those college musicals about the Big Game and the bestowing of a fraternity pin on the Homecoming Queen. A half-block north of the green and down a narrow alley is a head shop.

A head shop is where one buys the accessories of the psychedelic experience, grass pipes, for example, which are small pipes for smoking marijuana, and roach holders, which are elaborate clips for holding the tiny butt ends of marijuana cigarettes, or joints.

A few doors up the street, another establishment specializes in wall posters, beads and small brass Indian pipes for smoking hashish.

ROLL YOUR OWN

And the local stationery store, besides its stock of things like spiral notebooks, has a prominent display of Zig-Zag cigarette papers.

Nonetheless, no one was seen with the tag of a Bull Durham tobacco sack hanging out of his button-down shirt; the papers were for rolling joints.

In Cambridge, Mass., on a recent Friday, a dozen students at Harvard Law School gathered in an apartment for an evening of relaxation.

Four or five drew their chairs together and spoke of the possibility of political change in entrenched big-city bureaucracies. The others gathered about the fireplace and passed around a pipe, its bowl covered with perforated aluminum foil, and talked about movies, music and friends, and smoked marijuana.

"What the law school needs," said one future attorney, "is more snorts and less torts."

At a small Roman Catholic girls prep school outside San Francisco last spring, a local narcotics officer lectured on the danger of drugs. With many jocular remarks about making sure that he got them all back, he passed around three benzedrine pills and three marijuana cigarettes.

When they were returned, he humorously began to count them, and then discovered that he had got back four marijuana cigarettes.

In the late nineteen-sixties, a nationwide survey by The New York Times has found drugs, particularly marijuana, have become for many students a part of growing up, perhaps as common as the hip flasks of Prohibition.

HIPPIES AND THE MEDIA

While drug use has been expanding over the last few years, students and high school and college officials agree that it has increased sharply since the intensive coverage given to drugs and the hippies last summer by the mass media.

"There's no doubt this thing has increased since the summer. There were articles on the East Village in Esquire, Look and Life and this provides the image for the kids," said Dr. Donald W. Miles, the principal of Horace Greeley High School in the Westchester suburb of Chappaqua.

There does, in fact, appear to be far more drug use than police or academic officials say there is, and, particularly with marijuana, the drug use cuts across all types of young people.

In the past, younger students were introduced to drugs — "turned on" — by upperclassmen. Now, students on many campuses say freshmen arrive already smoking marijuana or taking it for granted that it is part of the college experience.

Marijuana — "grass" in the current campus phrase — has spread from avant-garde, artsy-craftsy colleges, through the Ivy League and the schools in big cities, through universities with transplanted New Yorkers, to campuses all over the country.

It also has spread to exclusive prep schools such as The Hun School in Princeton, N. J., and Phillips Academy in Andover, Mass., and on to high schools in places like Brattleboro, Vt., and Cedar Rapids, Iowa.

'MORE INTROSPECTIVE'

Dr. Kenneth Kenniston, assistant professor of psychology at the Yale University School of Medicine, could suggest to a recent meeting of the American Psychiatric Association that drug users were "largely congregated at the more selective, progressive and academically demanding institutions."

He also said they tended to be "better than average students," who majored "in the humanities, or perhaps in psychology," and were "rather more introspective than many of their classmates."

Most psychiatrists and administrators agree. They say that the student who uses drugs regularly tends to be rather bright and rather introspective, to often have deep personal or family problems, and to be alienated from both the values of the adult world and from those of his fellow students.

But, it is this type of students that psychiatrists and administrators are most likely to come in contact with, resulting in what sociologists term a "biased sample."

Interviews with students indicated that, while many drug takers appeared to be troubled, many did not

Furthermore, many students who gave little evidence of being particularly thoughtful seemed to be sampling drugs simply because they were available, or because they were considered sophisticated or daring. Others were smoking marijuana because it was the social thing to do, like sipping a cocktail.

A reporter for The Harvard Crimson, the undergraduate daily, recalled that four years ago a student turned in his roommate for smoking pot to "save" him.

"This would never happen today because the atmosphere has changed," he said. "It would be embarrassing for a student now to admit that he hadn't at least tried pot — just as it would be embarrassing for a Harvard student to admit that he was a virgin."

And, while a few years ago drug use appeared to be concentrated at better schools in the Northeast and on the West Coast, the scene is expanding rapidly.

The National Student Association collects newspaper articles about students arrested on drug charges. In the 24 cases listed for the first three weeks of last November, which were by no means all of them, there were arrests at Berkeley, Yale, New York University and the University of Wisconsin. There were also arrests at:

Franklin and Marshall College, Lancaster, Pa.; Hutchinson Community College, Hutchinson, Kan.; Piedmont College, Clarksville, Ga.; Towson State College, Towson, Md.; The University of Texas; Eastern New Mexico University in Portales; Pennsylvania Military College; Kansas Weslyan University in Salina; Northwestern University, Evanston, Ill.; Wichita State University in Wichita, Kan.; University of Nebraska; Michigan State University; Shimer College in Chicago; Eastern Illinois University in Charleston; Central Missouri State College in Warrensburg; Southern Illinois University in Carbondale. In the New York area there were arrests at Adelphi, Hofstra and the Collegiate Institute.

The survey showed that student comments about drugs, particularly marijuana, sound the same all over the country:

"It's not addicting. It's cheaper than booze and the high is better."

"When I'm high I'm in control of myself, when I'm drunk I'm not."

"There's no hangover."

"Man, when I'm high (snapping his fingers) ... like. I'm inside myself. I'm outside myself (snap, snap)."

"Why not?"

Despite this, there are distinctions among youthful drug users.

On the campuses, where drugs are a social experience, or perhaps an attempt at self-realization, they tend to be regarded earnestly, but only as a part of life. Among the hippie drop outs, they seem to be the focal point of existence.

In high schools, where a weird and dangerous variety of drugs may be taken without sophistication or discrimination, they are a remedy for boredom and a way of rebellion.

The most common mind-alerting drug used on campus, of course, is still alcohol. The drinking culture predominates, particularly at Southern universities, where the "foamies," beer drinkers, hold weekend binges, and at Roman Catholic institutions such as Fordham and St. John's, where vice tends to be more traditionally Irish.

THE 'HORROR SHOW'

A normal college weekend party is still marked by much ostentatious quaffing of beer or punch (usually a local specialty with a name like "Texas Twister" or "Purple Passion") or cheap bourbon.

There is also crowded dancing, spilled beer, big-beat rock 'n' roll, groping and pawing, passing out, throwing up, and maybe fights, smashed windows and furniture and occasional automobile accidents.

The activity, if it reaches the proper peak, is known on some campuses as a "horror show," and participants speak fondly of "throwing shows."

A drug party, in contrast, usually means a small group of friends — or sometimes only a boy and girl — in a dormitory room or, more likely, an off-campus apartment.

Perhaps there are candles burning, or perhaps incense to disguise the heavy, sweet odor of marijuana. The cigarette or pipe is passed quietly from person to person; each inhales deeply, holds his breath, and sniffs in more air to keep the smoke in the lungs.

As the light-headed, euphoric "high" comes on, there will be some giggles, some dangling conversation. They will listen to records — The Beatles, Bob Dylan, Ravi Shankar — talk, or simply sit and contemplate.

Later they will raid the icebox, or go to an all-night sandwich shop, for marijuana increases the appetite, and users say the sensation of taste is enhanced.

ALCOHOL IS YIELDING

Increasingly, the alcoholic party is yielding to this. At Colgate, for instance, one fraternity normally consumes ten kegs of beer on the big fall weekend when the houses are open to freshmen. This year it used only three.

At Amherst, a fraternity has switched almost completely to drugs, and others have found that their liquor bills have declined. A fraternity brother who was once known as "The Mad Dog" because of his behavior when he drank is now a pothead and is called "The Docile Dog."

Among younger pot smokers particularly, there is a strong revulsion toward alcohol. Young people who were graduated from college in the early sixties have discovered a generation gap as their younger brothers and sisters accuse them of ruining their health and losing their self-control by drinking.

"I just can't see drinking — pouring all those poisons into your body and becoming obnoxious, ugh," said a 17-year-old boy who goes to Hillhouse High School in New Haven and turns on nearly every weekend.

In contrast to marijuana, the use of acid — the hallucinogen LSD — has fallen off rapidly on most campuses. In some circles, however, it is being replaced with mescaline.

One major reason for the decline of LSD is the recent publicity about the possibility of hereditary defects and mutations from the drug. "I don't want any freaky three-headed kids," said one coed.

Another reason is that there have been too many "bad trips" and frightening experiences from taking LSD. Many students have found a trip too powerful and too exhausting an experience to repeat.

Still, many youths say that a trip has been a valuable experience — "I found out a lot about myself, including a lot of stuff I didn't like," is a common comment — and many of the bad trips have been unsettling rather than disastrous.

But everyone knows stories of people who took LSD and then leaped out of windows convinced they could fly, or attempted (sometimes with ghastly results) to stop rapidly moving traffic.

Or they know of experiences similar to that of a brilliant science student at Amherst who was dismissed from school a few months before his graduation.

On a bad trip, he had raced into the home of an elderly woman, screaming that the police were after him, and barricaded himself in a closet. The police weren't but they soon were.

Another problem with transparent tasteless LSD is the quality of the drug. Much of it has been cut with "speed" — methedrine, a powerful amphetamine — or other substances.

Amphetamines, in the form of benzedrine and dexedrine, have been used in colleges for years, not for kicks, but merely to stay awake, sometimes for days, while writing papers or taking exams.

This is not considered taking drugs, said a Harvard senior, "any more than No-Doz was in prep school."

But sometimes the results can be disastrous here, too. Some students have been hospitalized with exhaustion, and there is the case of the graduate student at the University of Oklahoma, who, stoked with dexedrine, walked out of an exam convinced he had written the best paper of his career.

He may well have, but no one will ever know, since he wrote it all on the same line.

While there are bizarre aspects to collegiate drug use — such as the students at Rice Institute in Texas who play "pill roulette" by grabbing an unidentified pill out of a paper sack on the way to class to find out what will happen when they take it — there are relatively few "stone heads," who center their lives on drugs.

"Most people go through three phases with drugs," explains a junior at the University of Massachusetts. "When you're first turned on, it's like the greatest thing in the world, and you get very evangelical; and run around talking about it all the time and trying to turn everybody else on.

"Then you go through a period when drugs are pretty important and you orient most of the rest of your life around the time when you turn on. Eventually there's just a lot of other stuff you want to do, so you just smoke once in a while."

Most experts, such as Dr. Joel Fort, who was once with the San Francisco Health Department, and Dr. Richard H. Blum, director of the Psychopharmacology Project of the Institute for the Study of Human Problems at Stanford University, agree that becoming "strung out" on drugs is not so much caused by the drug as it is the personality problems of the user.

This is backed up by such lay observations as that of a girl in Greenwich Village, who declared:

"Most of the real heads were completely freaked out before they ever saw dope; that bag is just their outlet."

DRUGS IN HIGH SCHOOL

Despite their apparent sophistication, many turned-on college students have been startled to find a widespread use of drugs at their old high schools, and some have been shocked by the abandon with which they are sampled.

"My 14-year-old sister, who goes to a nice Catholic girls' school, called me up this summer to tell me she'd been dropping STP [a hallucinogen] with the surfers on the Jersey shore," a 23-year-old pothead recalled. "I said, hold on, honey, we'd better have a little talk."

In Bethesda, Md., a suburb of Washington, members of the high school "blue glasses" hippie set have stolen whatever looked interesting from the medicine cabinets of homes where they were baby-sitting. The next day they see if anyone knows what it is. Then they take it to see what it does.

In Houston, teen-agers have told their parents they were going to the shore for the weekend, and then pooled their money and sent one of their number to San Francisco and back to fetch LSD.

In Beaverton, Ore., the largest suburb of Portland, half the students in a high school assembly raised their hands when asked if they knew where they could get marijuana. Two students there were arrested while shooting up methedrine in a restroom during a football game.

"The frightening thing about these kids is that they'll take anything, anywhere," said a young medical student at Yale, who is studying drug usage. "I used to think it wasn't so much different from what we did at that age, but this is really dangerous."

Indeed, it is the teenyboppers' ready acceptance of drugs such as methedrine, which can induce psychological dependence, compulsive, sometimes violent behavior and intense feelings of paranoia, which has hastened the break-up of the Haight-Ashbury hippie community in San Francisco.

The high school student most likely to use drugs, according to several high school principals, deans and suburban psychiatrists, is the bright student, who does not participate in school activities, who often has a troubled home life, and who feels alienated.

'A PERVASIVE DEPRESSION'

"One gets from these kids a feeling of nothingness, of pervasive depression," said Dr. H. R. Kormos, one of 14 psychiatrists in Westport, Conn., a wealthy suburb of 26,400 persons and 21 liquor stores.

"There is a very genuine feeling that life has little to offer them, and they speak continually of the dreariness, the drabness of everyday life," he said.

Dr. Kormos suggested that, particularly with marijuana, the mystique and ceremony of sharing the drug may impart a sense of belonging and identity that be more important to the student than the effect of the drug.

And, like other psychiatrists, school administrators and clergymen, Dr. Kormos spoke of the problems that an affluent society has created for young people: the shifting of families as businessmen are transferred about the country; the absence from home of a commuting, traveling father; the struggle for status and success; pressures to get into competitive colleges; and what the young person may see as a moral contradiction, Vietnam, for example.

"The drug problem is quite related to what's going on in the community; there's a lot of comment about the hypocrisy of the adult world," said the Rev. James G. Emerson Jr., who works with young people in weekly discussion sessions at the Larchmont Avenue Presbyterian Church in Larchmont, N.Y.

"These kids know a lot more; they're much more idealistic about life, and they feel they can't be idealistic in the church, in the school system or with their parents," he said.

"One of the real problems now is that parents over-react," Mr. Emerson continued. "Often a parent just latches on to the drugtaking and doesn't realize that it's really a symptom of other things."

One type of suburban student unlikely to use drugs, however, is the leather-jacketed "hood," who in past years might have been accused of creating teenage drinking or driving problems.

"These are usually the sons of the local tradespeople, and they're less articulate and resentful of the more affluent kids," a Westchester high school principal said.

"There's a real split here. The longhaired kids are against the war, for instance; these kids are for it. They view the drugs as a very moral issue. They've even beaten up some of the kids who were known to smoke marijuana."

The going rate for drugs varies with the area, the amount on the market and the source of supply, but an ounce of marijuana generally costs $15 to $20.

In some areas, users say, underworld elements have moved into the marijuana trade in the last few months and have driven prices up.

AN INFORMAL TRAFFIC

But for the most part the sources of drugs, particularly in colleges, are informal — normally a student who sells only to a small circle of friends, and usually not for a profit.

Probably the biggest carrier of drugs to campuses is the United States mail. There are some students, however, paying for their tuition or vacations, who make regular runs between Boston and New York, or who fly to San Francisco or drive to Mexico with an empty suitcase and back with a full one.

The unstructured nature of the traffic has posed a problem for the police. Increasingly they are planting undercover agents in high schools and colleges, and forcing students who have been arrested to turn informer.

In Washington County, Ore., outside of Portland, the chief of detectives in the county sheriffs office keeps a list of 400 teen-agers who are known or suspected users. In Madison, Wis., Detective Capt. Stanley Davenport says that 90 per cent of the students arrested cooperate with the police to avoid prosecution.

This troubles college administrators, who traditionally have stood somewhere between the students and the police. Most colleges are now issuing rather vaguely worded warnings about drugs, but most do not have a set policy, explaining that they prefer to deal with each case as it arises.

Pentagon Steps Up Fight on Drug Use in Vietnam

BY THE NEW YORK TIMES | FEB. 16, 1968

WASHINGTON, FEB. 15 — The Pentagon has stepped up efforts to stem the use of marijuana and other drugs by servicemen in Vietnam.

While stressing that the use of drugs in the armed forces is not a problem of "serious magnitude," officials said that marijuana smoking by servicemen had increased in the last two years not only in Vietnam but in the United States as well.

They had no estimates on the number of servicemen who have used marijuana, but statistics made available today show a sharp increase in the number of investigations conducted both in Vietnam and at home.

Figures show that 549 investigations into the use, possession and sale of marijuana by servicemen in Vietnam were conducted during the first six months of 1967, compared with 503 during all of 1966 and only 43 during 1965. Each investigation involves one serviceman.

While figures for all of 1967 are not yet complete, a preliminary tally indicates a total of 1,267 marijuana investigations in Vietnam, 1,118 involving Army troops, 64 involving sailors and marines, and 85 involving members of the Air Force.

These figures indicate an incidence of 2.5 investigations per thousand servicemen in Vietnam.

A total of 3,391 marijuana investigations were conducted among servicemen throughout the world in the first half of 1967, the figures show. This compares with 3,096 during all of 1966 and 522 during 1965.

More than half of these investigations were conducted among servicemen stationed in the United States.

Pentagon officials, while conceding there has been an increase in the use of marijuana by servicemen in Vietnam, say their figures are also the result of greater efforts to stem use of the drug.

Along with the statistics, officials also made available a directive on drug abuse issued on Feb. 2 by Paul H. Nitze, Deputy Secretary of Defense.

It outlines an enforcement and education program to curtail "illegal and improper use of drugs."

In addition, the directive calls for an identification of "areas and business establishments" where drugs are available so that they can be declared "off-limits" to servicemen.

Frank A. Bartimo, assistant general counsel for manpower and reserve affairs at the Pentagon, said military penalties for illegal drug use ranged from a simple warning to a general court-martial with the possibility of a dishonorable discharge.

He said special units of investigators, some involved in undercover work among servicemen concentrated on ferreting out suppliers among military personnel. He added, however, that there had been no evidence to suggest any organized attempt by the enemy or criminal elements to supply servicemen with drugs.

Some Vietnamese peasants, he said, earn small amounts selling marijuana to servicemen. The marijuana plant grows wild over most of Vietnam and is readily available.

The investigators, he said, are members of the military police and military intelligence units who have received training in drug investigations. Although he would not say how many men were involved in such activities, or give details on how they operate, other sources indicated that they numbered in the hundreds.

Mr. Bartimo said that in many cases their work involved investigations of black-market operations in other commodities besides drugs.

Marihuana Reconsidered

BY JAMES L. GODDARD | JUNE 27, 1971

POT USE "leads to violence and crime...opens the mind and enhances creativity...smoking is the first step in the use of such drugs as cocaine, morphine and heroin... is an aphrodisiac ... has a causal relationship to psychosis ... is an extremely safe drug when compared to secobarbital and alcohol."

Each of these partial quotations from Lester Grinspoon's recent book "Marihuana Reconsidered" can become the departure point for an evening — long discussion with one's friends, reaffirming for the cognoscenti the suspicion that demonologists are in our midst. Having tilted on numerous occasions with those whose minds have been captured by the "demonology" of marijuana I am particularly sensitive to how deeply we as a society have been committed to a position that is based on superstition and undocumented hearsay. For three generations misinformation about this drug has been embedded into our literature, our minds, our ethos and, increasingly, our laws.

How well this misinformation has been planted and carefully nurtured is attested to by our continued inability to use the available scientific evidence to modify Federal statutes which are not only unrealistic but Draconian in nature. This societal "blindspot" has created a dilemma. One facet of the dilemma is the Alice-in-Wonderland relationship we have fashioned between marijuana and alcohol.

On the one hand we find that possession of alcohol, a central nervous system depressant which has produced physical dependence in an estimated 6,000,000 Americans and psychological dependence in perhaps five times that number, is not only free of penalty but its use is even encouraged by our society to such a degree that nonusers of the drug are regarded by most as being somewhat peculiar. On the other hand mere possession of marijuana, a mild "hallucinogen" incapable of producing physical dependence and whose ability to create psychological dependence is judged to be less than that of alcohol and tobacco, is considered a heinous crime punishable upon conviction by imprisonment for varying periods up to 99 years.

Grinspoon, a Harvard Medical School psychiatrist, analyzes this and other aspects of the marijuana problem and concludes that, "we must consider the enormous harm, both obvious and subtle, short range and long-term, inflicted on the people, particularly the young, who constitute or will soon constitute the formative and critical members of our society by the present punitive, repressive approach to the use of marijuana. And we must consider the damage inflicted on legal and other institutions when young people react to what they see as a confirmation of their view that those institutions are hypocritical and inequitable. Indeed the greatest potential for social harm lies in the scarring of so many young people and the reactive, institutional damages that are direct products of present marijuana laws. If we are to avoid having this harm reach the proportion of a national disaster within the next decade, we must move to make the social use of marijuana legal."

Before reaching this conclusion Grinspoon covers, in an unusually well documented fashion, the biology, chemistry, pharmacology and toxicity of marijuana; the potential medical uses which merit further study; the psychological effects of using the drug; and the social and legal implications of usage both with regard to the individual and society. For the serious student who seeks original sources a 42-page section of notes has been provided.

That there will be criticisms of the conclusions and the manner in which they were reached goes without question, for the issues involved are so emotionally laden that reason will be cast aside and specious arguments introduced. There will be critics who will find fault on the grounds that the potential dangers have been minimized and that we know too little to legalize usage at this point in time. Others will argue that undue bias was involved in the exclusion of reports which document the problems associated with usage of cannabis sativa (marijuana).

As to the first criticism the author in anticipation states, "it is quite true that among the hundreds and hundreds of papers dealing with cannabis, there is relatively little methodologically sound research. Yet out of this vast collection of largely unsystematic recordings comes the strong impression that no amount of research is likely to prove that cannabis is as dangerous as alcohol and tobacco." On this point I would agree that research may not be able to demonstrate equivalent dangers, but I would hasten to point out if usage were at the same level and over as prolonged a period of time we might find that lung cancer, or emphysema or other disorders would occur as often as with tobacco. This does not invalidate Grinspoon's conclusions but rather suggests that if the use of marijuana were to be made legal it should be made available in dosage forms that are potentially less dangerous.

On the second point concerning the bias in selection of material, having personally reviewed the English portion of the world literature in preparation for Congressional hearings, I can only express my admiration for the manner in which Grinspoon has extracted, analyzed and synthesized the most relevant literature to present the reader with a coherent, logical case. He inevitably leads to the conclusion that, as a society, we were systematically coerced into making the same mistake in 1937 with marijuana that was made earlier with alcohol by the passage of the Volstead Act.

It is difficult to understand why this "error" was made by many of the same legislators who just a few years earlier had in repealing the Volstead Act recognized the wisdom of Spinoza's admonition: "He who seeks to regulate everything by law is more likely to arouse vices than reform them." Difficult, at any rate, unless one speculates that the liquor lobby played a critical, albeit subtle role in the "legal onslaught" which occurred during the early and mid-thirties and culminated in the passage of the Federal Marijuana Tax Act of 1937.

Knowing something of the inner workings of Federal regulatory agencies, this speculation, which Grinspoon notes in his especially interesting first chapter, "The History of Marihuana in the United

States," is not an implausible one and on several occasions in the past the press has pointedly ignored my suggestion that the archives be searched for evidence to support the thesis that alcohol was "protected" against the burgeoning menace of the "killer drug, marijuana" during the post-repeal era of the 1930's. Such a finding would, however, have little effect today other than to strengthen the suspicions held by many of the young generation concerning the Establishment and its illogical positions on drugs in society.

Why and how such positions could occur is dealt with by the author in his all too brief discussion of the "possible" causes of our attitudes to marijuana, LSD and amphetamines. Grinspoon believes that a displacement phenomena operates within our society: "...people may unconsciously transfer affect from its real object to substitute objects." Thus our concern about nuclear holocausts, environmental pollution, social instability, crowding and population may be displaced by attaching affect to substitute issues, such as drugs. If true, this provides partial explanation for the unwillingness of Congress to listen to knowledgeable witnesses who have counseled against repressive legislation and subsequent Congressional reluctance to take cognizance of evidence clearly indicating the need for change.

One group opposing the passage of the 1937 Act outlawing marijuana was The American Medical Association. The opposition was based on concern that the act would not accomplish its objectives, would be unnecessarily expensive for the physicians to comply with and that the drug should continue to be available for restudy by modern means — such studies they believed could show "other advantages to be obtained from its medicinal use." Their concern with the ineffectiveness of the act has proven to be well founded. Less well appreciated is the fact that research was for all practical purposes completely stifled for over 30 years. Fortunately that situation has now been remedied, and we are now well into the efforts to derive therapeutically useful substances from the very complex constituents which make up the marijuana plant.

Grinspoon's evaluation is that new products may be developed from either naturally occurring marijuana or one of the synthetic forms which have: (1) analgesic properties in combination with mood elevating abilities; (2) the effect of lowering blood pressure through different mechanisms than today's drugs; and (3) have antidepressant and antianxiety effects again different in their mechanism of action than today's drugs. Emergence of a new drug in any one of these three classes would be a substantial contribution, particularly if the drug possessed greater margins of safety or fewer side effects than drugs presently being used.

The development of a new drug, no matter how valuable, would of course not change the major issue for the 20 million or so users in our society today. They will continue to press for legalization of marijuana in the face of opposition from the majority of the citizenry, who although ill-informed and overactive, feel that to take this step "would be to invite national tragedy."

As for myself, I would favor legalization only if I were confident that a control system could be devised to preclude widespread usage by adolescents. They are not well equipped to handle a drug which provides a pleasant escape from reality, promotes inattention and would distract them from their main task — growing up. But hopefully many Americans will read Lester Grinspoon's "Marihuana Reconsidered" and utilize the information so well presented in reaching their own decision on "pot," to legalize or not.

'Decriminalizing' Marijuana

EDITORIAL | BY THE NEW YORK TIMES | FEB. 20, 1972

IS "POT" HARMFUL? Classified as a "narcotic drug" by law, with severe penalties imposed for its sale, use or mere possession, marijuana has been treated as an extremely harmful commodity at all levels of government for many years. Only during the last few years, however, has the medical profession closely studied marijuana. The validity of the law depends on the answer to the question: How harmful is "pot"? That answer is only now beginning to come in.

According to both the National Institute of Mental Health and the National Commission on Marijuana and Drug Abuse, the dangers inherent in smoking marijuana appear to be less than previously assumed. On the basis of recent medical inquiry, both studies have now supported "decriminalization" of marijuana. This is a tentative interim step that would separate marijuana from hard, addictive drugs like heroin and would place the weight of law somewhere between the current stiff sanctions and outright legalization. It is a step suggested only for marijuana and not for the hard drugs.

Dr. Bertram S. Brown, director of N.I.M.H., says flatly that marijuana penalties are "much too severe and much out of keeping with knowledge about its harmfulness." The national commission, appointed by President Nixon specifically to study the issue, has prepared a formal report due for release soon which also recommends abolition of all criminal penalties for private use and possession of marijuana.

This double recommendation from such authoritative sources should have influence not only on Congress but also on state legislatures, such as New York's, currently wrestling with proposals to change the drug laws. A New York legislative committee last year recommended reclassification of marijuana — now a "narcotic drug" under New York law — and reduction of penalties associated with it. Mere possession of marijuana remains a "class A" misdemeanor in this state, punishable by as much as one year in jail. If one college student gives another a marijuana cigarette — something that appears to happen frequently on college campuses — he may be subject to as much as 25 years in jail.

Fortunately, these penalties are seldom imposed by a generally enlightened New York State judiciary; but their existence on the statute books is now anachronistic. Neither the N.I.M.H. nor the national commission seems prepared at this point to advocate outright legalization of marijuana; the accumulation of further medical evidence might justify such a step later on.

What is immediately called for is a sharp scaling down of marijuana penalties, elimination of criminal sanctions for its use or possession and reduction penalties for its small-quantity sales. A failure of legislatures to base legal sanctions on the best medical evidence available can only undermine respect for the law.

Marijuana Study by U.S. Finds No Serious Harm

BY WALTER SULLIVAN | JULY 9, 1975

A FEDERALLY CONTRACTED study of marijuana smoking in Jamaica, where the consumption by heavy users is said to be 10 to 25 times that of their American counterparts, has failed to confirm any serious adverse effects.

The only significant difference found between smokers and nonsmokers was that among smokers there was a slightly higher incidence of hypoxia, or reduced delivery of oxygen, to tissues by the bloodstream.

It was suspected, however, that this may result from the use of tobacco, which is customarily mixed with the marijuana by Jamaicans.

The study was done for the Center for Studies of Narcotic and Drug Abuse of the National Institute of Mental Health. It was directed by Drs. Vera Rubin and Lambros Comitas of the Research Institute for the Study of Man at 162 East 78th Street in New York.

Participating as well were the University of the West Indies and 35 physicians, psychiatrists, other specialists and staff members.

The report of its findings, in book form, became available last week. At the same time the Drug Abuse Council, an independent, Washington-based organization, reported the findings of 19 experts who met in January to assess various attempts to determine the risks of marijuana use.

SIGNIFICANCE OF CHANGES

They agreed that smoking the herb can bring about certain bodily changes but said the significance of those changes was uncertain.

"Large-scale epidemiological investigations similar to those which established associations between smoking cigarettes and health hazards will be required to identify certain health consequences of chronic marijuana use," said a summary of the drug council's findings.

"Since these studies of intensive, long-term marijuana consumers have not been done," it added, "our knowledge of the drug's chronic effects is still limited." The council was set up in 1972 by the Ford Foundation and three other foundations to provide independent guidance in coping with drug abuse.

In a foreword to the Jamaican study, Raymond Philip Shafer, who headed President Nixon's National Commission on Marijuana and Drug Abuse, hailed it as "the first intensive, multidisciplinary study of marijuana use to be published."

He cited a comment by Oliver Wendell Holmes former United States Supreme Court Justice that dragons in dark caves are far more fearsome than in daylight. It is therefore refreshing, he wrote, to have "an objective study which not only exposes but demolishes many emotional and 'fright-symbolic' dragons" regarding marijuana use.

Mr. Sharer, a law school classmate of President Ford and former Governor of Pennsylvania, is now an aide to Vice President Rockefeller.

In 1973 his drug abuse commission recommended abolition of penalties for private use of and possession of marijuana, but this was not welcomed by President Nixon.

CONTRADICTIONS ARE NOTED

The Jamaican report is discussed by Dr. Erich B. Goode, associate professor of sociology at the State University of New York in Stony Brook, in the July 4 issue of Science. It is, he writes, "one of the most significant sets of findings on cannabis ever assembled in a single study."

Cannabis is the scientific name of the plant genus from which marijuana is derived. Dr. Goode is an authority on its effects and is clearly in sympathy with the report's findings. He notes that they contradict earlier reports of chromosome damage, loss of the ability to combat disease, brain damage and loss of motivation derived from marijuana use.

On Tuesday, for example, this newspaper published a letter on the subject by Dr. Gabriel Nahas and several others at Columbia University's College of Physicians and Surgeons.

"Recent medical evidence," they wrote, "indicates that long-term marijuana smoking in amounts currently used in the U.S. is associated with the following hazards:

"Hormonal imbalance, inhibition of spermatogenesis, lung damage, impairment of immunity, increased formation of chromosome deficient cells with possible damage to the offspring, interference with memory and speech and impairment of driving performance."

The evidence for immunity impairment was reported in 1973 by Dr. Nahas and his colleagues in Science. Last April, in the same journal, a group from the Veterans Administration Hospital in Washington, D.C., reported findings that "differ completely" from those of Dr. Nahas.

In evaluating such research the Drug Abuse Council's summary states that marijuana "can impair" that component of the human immune response mediated by one type of white blood cell (the T cell). "But," it continues, "it is unclear what significance this alteration has for the total immune response and hence for the susceptibility to disease."

Jamaica was chosen for the study because of the high rate of marijuana consumption in a sociological setting basically different from that in the United States. Instead of being socially frowned upon, it is generally accepted, with the nonuser being regarded as the nonconformist.

It is not used in a recreational context but as an "energizer" for those doing heavy work. Studies based on videotapes and other recording devices showed that workers performed better when using cannabis than when not doing so.

Fear in the United States that such use leads to lethargy "is not borne out by the life histories of Jamaican working-class subjects or by objective measurements," the report says. These, it adds, indicate that heavy use "does not diminish work drive or work ethic."

Furthermore, it says, "There is no evidence of any causal relationship between cannabis use and mental deterioration, insanity, violence or poverty." The only medical differences found between smokers and nonsmokers were circulatory and lung effects that could be attributed to tobacco.

The Drug Abuse Council summary reflects a similar assessment. The experts found "no definite evidence" of mental illness, persistent loss of motivation or brain damage. However they gave more credence to evidence of an effect on the synthesis of DNA (the key substance of the genetic process).

This did not necessarily represent any threat to human genetics or reproduction, they said, but added: "Since marijuana easily crosses the placental barrier, the use of marijuana by pregnant women is especially unwise."

EFFECT ON SEX HORMONE

The summary also notes that "under certain conditions" use of the herb reduces levels of testosterone, the male sex hormone, but again, it said, the significance of this was unclear.

While further health hazards will probably be identified, the summary added, "Our present state of knowledge indicates that, although there are always ample reasons to be concerned about the use of any drug, there are no new reasons to be especially disturbed by the use of marijuana."

Nor was there evidence that the users tended to become inured and turn to other drugs. Hard drug usage is low. Furthermore Mr. Shafer suggests that the use of marijuana cuts down on alcoholism.

Alcoholics account for less than one per cent of mental hospital admissions in Jamaica, whereas in other Caribbean areas where the herb is little used, admissions of alcoholics run as high as 55 per cent.

In his review Dr. Goode says that "only by examining the use of a drug in a wide range of settings and environments can we piece together anything like a well-rounded picture of what it does to people."

"For most drugs," he adds, "what we know comes from studies on a narrow range of subjects — usually American, and usually 'captive' prison, hospital or college populations." He says that, while marijuana is technically outlawed in Jamaica, its use is so widely accepted that the study could be done there far more readily than in the United States.

The Jamaican report is entitled "Ganja in Jamaica," ganja being the term for marijuana used on that island. It is a Hindi word as use of the herb was introduced by East Indian laborers in the nineteenth century. The Jamaican marijuana appears to be a more potent form than the Mexican variety familiar to Americans.

The report says that whereas the typical American user consumes only one or two marijuana cigarettes a week, a moderate Jamaican users smokes the equivalent of five to eight a day. A heavy Jamaican user was said to smoke in excess of eight a day. Because the Jamaican herb is more potent, the Jamaican user's intake of the active ingredient was said to be 10 to 25 times that of his American counterpart.

According to the report, the Jamaican users raised the suggestion that many of the effects reported by the American users may be

BETTMANN/GETTY IMAGES

A section of leaves from a wild marijuana plant is held up for close inspection in a field west of Kearney, Neb. Law enforcement authorities in Nebraska's Buffalo County use an airplane to spot "crops" of the "weed."

subjective. Few of the Jamaicans reported the sensations described by American users, such as a sharpening of taste, enhanced hearing and appreciation of music or loss of a sense of elapsed time.

A variety of medical and psychological tests were performed on matched groups of 30 smokers and 30 nonsmokers. However, it was difficult to find as many as 30 who had never smoked cannabis. Chronic users were asked not to smoke while in a hospital for the tests, and no withdrawal symptoms were observed.

While in-depth medical examinations were given to each subject, some of the effects, such as allegedly impaired sperm production, were not tested as they had not been reported when the two-year project was began in 1970.

The report, published by Mouton at the Hague in the Netherlands, is being distributed by MacFarland Publications of Scotch Plains, N.J.

Mr. Shafer did not contend that marijuana is entirely safe. "There are always risks inherent in the use of any 'drug,' including aspirin," he wrote. To what extent a harmful effect "is inherent in the substance and to what extent in the society or in the consumer is the research problem that must be divorced from spurious issues, especially in the case of marijuana."

"Everyone agrees," he concluded, that "continuing research and evaluation are necessary."

Marijuana as Medicine

EDITORIAL | BY THE NEW YORK TIMES | JULY 17, 1978

STUDENTS OF IRONY might dwell on the availability of marijuana. Every high school student knows how to get it — or knows someone else who does. Its aroma hangs over audiences at rock concerts. Some 35 million Americans have tried the drug and perhaps 11 million use it regularly. Yet those who need it for medical reasons are often unable to obtain it: marijuana has not yet passed the Food and Drug Administration's stringent requirements for use as a prescription drug. Now, however, four states — New Mexico, Florida, Illinois and Louisiana — have passed laws to encourage therapeutic use, generally as part of a "research" program.

At present, patients must go to extraordinary lengths to obtain marijuana legally. Consider the District of Columbia man who needed the drug to keep from going blind. He was arrested for growing his own supply, then had to spend $10,000 in a legal fight to obtain the drug. He eventually made a persuasive case: tests at leading universities showed marijuana could save his sight while conventional medications could not. So the Government agreed to supply him with marijuana cigarettes, and a court dismissed the charges against him. But even this treatment is being provided under a "research" project in which he happens to be the sole subject. Thus are the rules bent to accommodate a tenacious patient.

Marijuana shows great, but not fully proven, potential as a therapeutic agent. It eases pressure within the eyes of glaucoma victims. It reduces or eliminates the nausea, vomiting and loss of appetite in some cancer patients undergoing chemotherapy. It appears to help the breathing of asthmatics. It may also be useful against epilepsy, alcoholism and multiple sclerosis, and as a sedative or antidepressant. And compared with many other drugs, it is relatively safe.

Marijuana boosters want it legalized immediately for widespread medical use. That would be premature. The need now is for accelerated research to define its medical value. Yet progress has been greatly slowed by the drug's lingering notoriety. Marijuana is now classified under Federal drug laws in the most restrictive category — one reserved for highly dangerous drugs that have no accepted medical use.

The situation seems to be loosening up. The National Organization for the Reform of Marijuana Laws, and other petitioners, have, with the help of the Federal courts, forced the Government to consider placing marijuana and its derivatives in less restrictive legal categories. A committee of experts impaneled by the Food and Drug Administration has recommended that two chemical components of marijuana be reclassified. That would lessen the drug's stigma and make it easier to conduct research.

More important, a change in official attitudes has been signaled from the White House. Dr. Peter Bourne, special assistant to the President on health issues, has urged Federal agencies to consider the therapeutic value of all drugs — including marijuana and the much more dangerous heroin — purely on their medical and scientific merits. That puts the emphasis where it belongs — on a drug's medical potential rather than its political notoriety.

Research on Marijuana Finds Many Risks, Some Benefits

BY HAROLD M. SCHMECK JR. | OCT. 9, 1979

MORE POTENT TYPES of marijuana and alarmingly greater use among young teen-agers require a new attitude of concern toward the substance, some experts believe.

"The rules of the game have been changed," said Dr. Sidney Cohen of the University of California at Los Angeles, former head of Federal drug abuse research.

Imported marijuana used today is often 10 times as potent as the domestic "pot" smoked a few years ago, he said. Many Americans use it more heavily and the age at which use begins is dropping toward 12 to 14 years. At this formative age, dependence on any powerful substance — alcohol, tobacco, even coffee — is viewed with concern by health experts.

More than 43 million Americans have tried marijuana, according to the latest surveys, and almost half that number may be regular users.

Research over the past several years has suggested that marijuana has deleterious effects on vital bodily functions. And new findings continue to hint of marijuana's effects on the body. But the evidence remains inconclusive and, in any case, most researchers agree that moderate, occasional smoking is probably no significant hazard to physically and mentally healthy adults who are not pregnant.

There is also accumulating evidence that marijuana has potential medical uses. Foremost among these are reduction of excessive eye pressure in glaucoma and lessening of the nausea caused by powerful anti-cancer drugs. There are also suggestions that one or another ingredient in marijuana might be useful as a muscle relaxant.

"A recurrent problem this year as well as last is the limited number of new findings available to shed light on questions badly needing illumination, but for which definitive answers are elusive," said the latest marijuana report by the National Institute on Drug Abuse.

This uncertainty, specialists say, adds to the problem of frank disbelief by many young people that "pot" has any dangers. Lurid accounts of alleged hazards a decade ago left a legacy of skepticism.

Clearly, however, there are powerful and complex immediate effects. The most obvious is the psychological "high" for which marijuana has been famous for 4,000 years. It also raises heart rate, distorts perceptions and hampers the psychomotor skills needed for driving and operating machinery. These skills involve physical coordination, quick reaction time and visual perception.

As to the multitude of possible health effects, Federal experts and advisers list nine current areas of concern. In addition to known effects on psychomotor skills these are possible harm to lungs, heart, hormone production, immunity, genetics, and three related categories of effects on mind and brain.

The list itself shows the complexity of marijuana and its potential effects as well as the often contradictory results of research.

"The cannabinoids are biologically incredibly active substances," said Dr. Reese T. Jones of the University of California, San Francisco. This makes them both fascinating and an important subject of study, he said, but also makes the research difficult.

In this family of chemicals called cannabinoids, the one principality involved in the "high" is delta-9-tetrahydrocannabinol. It is known as THC. Scientists who have studied marijuana say the chemicals are a potent but elusive class apart from other substances known to affect brain and other body systems. They defy prediction from experience with other drugs.

Recently several key scientists and others of widely disparate views have reached a consensus that some groups should definitely avoid the drug in the light of the research findings. Among those groups are persons in the middle teens and younger, heart patients, pregnant women, persons with lung disease and anyone who appears prone to emotional disturbances. It was also agreed that driving an auto after smoking marijuana can be hazardous. The National Institute on Drug Abuse is circulating a letter to broaden adherence to that consensus to include a wide range of public figures and then plans to publicize the consensus statement widely.

The statement stems from recent testimony by Dr. Cohen of U.C.L.A. before a Congressional committee. It gains importance from the fact that its first adherents include such sharply opposed commentators on marijuana as the National Organization for the Reform of Marijuana Laws (NORML) and Dr. Gabriel G. Nahas of Columbia University, a specialist in marijuana research who has been one of the most outspoken scientists in warning of dangers in its use.

Many statements on the subject are as much political as scientific, some participants in the discussions say, asserting that the statements reflect social attitudes toward drugs in general as much as any specific knowledge of marijuana's effects.

"The whole country is shifting toward a more conservative, authoritarian mood," says Dr. David Zinberg, a psychiatrist of Harvard University. "As always, drugs make a nice scapegoat." The trend that he considers a legitimate cause for worry, however, is the downward shift in age of first use.

This age trend is also the main basis for present sharp concern about marijuana in the Carter Administration, according to Lee I. Dogoloff, associate director for drug policy of the White House domestic policy staff. His group is assembling a major public education program on teen-age drug abuse to counter the trend.

The very fact that a long list of possible effects of marijuana on the body can be drawn may distort public perception of the facts by implying that there is in fact damage to all these vital systems. But in many cases the supporting data are controversial. Throughout the drug institute's report on human effects the words "contradictory," "uncertain," "unevaluated," and "unconfirmed," run like a minor theme. "A continuing problem throughout the past decade has been the tendency to over interpret preliminary research findings," said the report.

Yet, in light of marijuana's wide use, the possibilities cannot safely be ignored.

"We are very concerned about the health hazards of marijuana use," said Dr. William Pollin, director of the National Institute on Drug Abuse, in testimony before the House Select Committee on Narcotics Abuse and Control.

He listed the major areas of concern, giving the Government's current appraisal of the state of knowledge on each.

For instance, he pointed out, virtually all studies of performance while "high" support the view that marijuana interferes with immediate memory and such intellectual necessities as reading comprehension, arithmetic problem-solving and thinking in general, he said.

Similarly there is agreement concerning the ill effects on driving ability.

The evidence is also considered strong that heart rate increases under the influence of marijuana. In healthy young adults this effect would probably be harmless, but it might well harm persons who have poor circulation of blood to the heart muscle. This danger has made possible the emerging consensus that marijuana is unsafe for heart patients.

Most American users of marijuana take it by smoking. The grim conclusions concerning tobacco smoking over the past several decades have raised similar fears of lung damage and perhaps cancer from marijuana. As with tobacco there are potentially cancer-causing chemicals in the "tar." As with cigarette smoking, it may take decades for a cancer risk to become obvious. The research to date leaves this a "serious concern," according to the Federal assessment.

Paradoxically some research has suggested marijuana may be useful in short-term treatment of an important breathing problem — asthma, because the drug acts as a dilator of small airway passages. Some believe, however, that the smoke's long-term irritating effects would probably cancel out that possible benefit.

EFFECTS ON IMMUNE SYSTEM

There has been evidence, from research in humans and animals, that marijuana may have harmful effects on the immunological defense system, but the practical implications of this remain in doubt.

Noting that there have been reports of damage to chromosomes, the Federal monograph said there is "no convincing evidence" that these are significant for human health "although the possibility cannot be completely dismissed." Much the same lack of proof was cited concerning previous reports of brain damage from heavy exposure to marijuana.

Effects on hormone production, including the male sex hormone testosterone, have also been reported.

"For those who want to worry, there is a lot more to worry about there," said Dr. Jones. "The animal data are just overwhelming that there are various endocrine abnormalities." His group's work at the University of California shows decreases in human testosterone, but these decreases still left the levels within the normal range.

Dr. Nahas of Columbia says marijuana's active ingredients affect the hypothalamus of the brain and, through this action, can have effects on the pituitary gland and many of the hormones that affect development and reproductive functions. He believes the evidence grows continually stronger.

CHAPTER 3

1980s–90s: The U.S. Government's "War on Drugs"

If the 1960s and '70s were defined by the counterculture and its embrace of cannabis, the 1980s and '90s were marked by the U.S. government's War on Drugs and a push to limit the trafficking and use of cannabis. Extensive education campaigns focused on deterring students from its use, while harsh sentencing laws jailed dealers and those in possession of cannabis. Disproportionate numbers of African-Americans and Latinos populated courts and jails, revealing a stark double standard in how society dealt with cannabis users.

New Parental Push Against Marijuana

BY ELISABETH COLEMAN BRYNNER | FEB. 10, 1980

A dramatic increase in the use of pot by teen-agers and young children has parents all over the country revving up for the antidrug battle.

"I CRIED FOR A WEEK," Ednis Smith said. She had found a marijuana pipe in the wash with her daughter's blue jeans. "I just stayed at home and wept. How could I explain to people that my beautiful 18-year-old daughter had been on pot ever since she was in junior high?" Mrs. Smith is a Mormon, a rancher's wife, in the town of Enumclaw in the state of Washington, and she didn't stay home for long. She spoke up at a school meeting called to discuss drug problems, and she helped to organize a parents' group devoted to combating marijuana. She has just finished a primer on the subject intended for grammar-school children.

During the last few years, hundreds of such antipot parents' organizations have sprung up, unheralded, around the nation. Not for these men and women the notion of marijuana as a mild and pleasant alternative to the martini, a weekend reminder of the 1960's when marijuana was an adolescent emblem of peace and love. Their children are part of a new generation of young pot smokers who start at an earlier age, smoke grass more than 10 times as strong and light up before, after and during school hours. And parents, whether or not they themselves have smoked pot, tend to react with anger and fear when their children start to show some of the typical side effects of heavy smoking — the loss of interest in schoolwork, the changed emotional set toward life in general and toward the family in particular.

The backlash against pot shows up in national polls: For the first time in a decade, the percentage of Americans favoring the legalization of marijuana has begun to drop — from 28 percent in a 1977 Gallup poll to 25 percent in 1978. It finds concrete expression in a model law against paraphernalia outlets, released by the Federal Government Nov. 1; in the creation of special displays on marijuana in public libraries; in a harder line toward pot on the part of local communities and some school administrators.

ONE REASON for the public upset is the amazing growth of heavy marijuana use among school-age children. A national survey of high-school seniors last year, for example, showed that one out of every nine got high at least once a day — twice the figure for 1975. (For the purposes of this article, a "pothead," a "heavy" smoker, is one who uses a minimum of one joint a day.) Just as significant, experts say, is the degree to which pot has invaded the lower age groups. Statewide surveys in Maine and Maryland, for instance, indicated that one of every six youngsters in all grades of high school smoked grass daily. Moreover, the recent and dramatic increase in public awareness of the ill effects of heavy smoking on children's minds and bodies has added fuel to the antipot fire, and the issue was dramatically underlined in testimony by health experts at United States Senate hearings last month.

The new breed of young pothead is very different from the "flower child" of a decade ago.

On an unseasonably warm November afternoon, on a park bench near the West 93d Street entrance to Manhattan's Central Park, three 16-year-old girls take time out from their rollerskating to roll a joint. They are all students at a nearby parochial school, and they say they have been smoking since sixth grade. One of the girls takes a few hits; her eyes redden and a flush spreads across the bridge of her nose. Just then her French teacher walks by, and they exchange greetings.

The next day, at the Riverdale Junior High School in the Bronx, hundreds of children pour out the door, blinking in the sunlight, for their lunch break. It becomes evident that literally dozens of them are stoned. One 14-year-old, who keeps trying to slap a baggy purse against her leg, but often misses, answers questions:

Why does she smoke grass?

"Yeah, I'm stoned. We ... get ... spaced-doo-dee."

Doo-dee?

"Doo-dee, yaah."

How long has she been smoking pot?

"Three."

Three what?

"Three." She holds up two fingers, unsteadily adds a third and wanders off.

Late one afternoon in the Bedford Record Shop in Stamford, Conn., two boys, 14 years of age, examine the array of glass and plastic water pipes, or "bongs," and then move on to counters covered by garish bowls and roach clips (to permit smoking of the last fragment of a joint) and tubes and other pot paraphernalia. They pause beside the fake Diet Pepsi cans with the glass container for grass inside. One of the two young customers, whose teeth are hidden behind a solid wall of braces, settles on a facsimile of an M-16 shell that is, in fact, a roach clip. "Have fun, guys," says the shopkeeper as he puts the purchase into a brown paper bag. "No one will ever guess."

On an upper-middle-class street in Atlanta, a tow-haired sixth-grader checks to see whether his parents are watching, then loads up the special compartment built under his skate-board. His cargo: "loose joints" (single joints) and "nickel bags" and "dime bags" (plastic bags holding $5 and $10 worth of loose marijuana). He and other bike-and-skateboard entrepreneurs like him in even lower grades sometimes clear $100 a week.

Pot smoking and dealing have moved down through the school grades and age levels and have become an integral part of the experience of growing up. Says David Moxhay, dean of students at Greenwich High School in Connecticut: "Several years ago, high-school students were experimenting. Now we are finding that in most cases people coming into high school may have started using it in fourth, fifth or sixth grade, and got into a heavy dependence by junior-high school."

Sometimes older siblings perform the introduction. One reason, says Barry Wilansky, executive director of TEMPO, a drug rehabilitation program for children in Long island, "is to keep the younger ones from ratting on them. But of course they are also maintaining their adulthood in the eyes of their younger brothers and sisters, and doing a kind of parenting."

More often, a friend presides over the initiation. According to Robert L. DuPont, president of the Institute for Behavior and Health and former head of the National Institute on Drug Abuse (NIDA), "the single main determinant of whether a particular young person uses drugs like marijuana is whether his best friend uses or doesn't use it. "

But youngsters themselves tell of a wide variety of sponsors. A 16-year-old Manhattan girl laughingly remembers being taken out for a canter by her instructor at a riding camp in Pennsylvania and turned on to pot at age 14. A young man in Connecticut tells how his high-school wrestling coach used to turn on with him and another student before a match. Stories are rife of school-bus drivers who not only permit smoking but sell pot to their passengers.

The attractions of pot for younger children are multiple and, to some degree, familiar. They like the way it makes them feel, the way it makes big problems seem small and smaller problems nonexistent. Because it has become so much a part of the school scene, marijuana attracts children with special needs. "If a youngster doesn't belong to a group," says one educator, "if he's new to the school or lonely, all he has to do is light up a joint and he's instantly adopted by somebody."

For the younger potheads in particular, the whole culture that surrounds marijuana has a special attraction: the equipment, the language, the secrecy. "It's a game," says Robert Kramer, director of the Office of Alcohol and Drug Abuse in Anne Arundel County, Md. "And the game is, 'We will use drugs and conceal them, right under your noses.' "

Dealing is a big part of the game and, for many, a necessary part. A loose joint, generally made with an inferior grade of marijuana, has a street price of about a dollar. Most students roll their own, using pot that costs from $50 an ounce up to as much as $125 an ounce; a single joint will still cost close to a dollar, but it will be stronger and better tasting.

Some children pay for pot out of their allowances or their lunch money, or take jobs after school. Others depend upon the largess of friends. But heavy smokers tend to deal, for fun and profit. David Moxhay says that high-school students in the Greenwich area make thousands of dollars a year dealing in grass, alone. A Long Island student tells of supporting his 6-to-10-joint-a-day habit during his sophomore year in high school: "I'd deal anywhere and everywhere — in the bathroom, the hall, outside or even through the window of a class in progress. It's easy. It's funny."

A time-honored means of keeping in pot is petty theft. The children dip into their parents' wallets and pocketbooks. (A New Jersey mother says she took to sleeping with her purse under her pillow after catching her 14-year-old pot-head son with his hand in her wallet.) They learn to shoplift and break into mailboxes, and where to sell the goods. One youngster in Riverdale said that while another gang in the area broke into cars to raise funds for pot, he and his buddies "ran over little old ladies and stole their purses."

Studies have not, however, established a direct cause-and-effect relationship between marijuana smoking and youthful crime — or, for that matter, between marijuana and truancy or suicide. Most young truants and vandals smoke dope, but there is no clear proof that they would not have been truants and vandals without it.

EVIDENCE OF MARIJUANA'S effects upon the minds and bodies of the young is easier to come by. The backlash against pot among parents reflects, in part, their increased perception of these dangers. Even such advocates of pot as Andy Kowal, publisher of The Accessories Digest, acknowledge its impact upon children. "My personal opinion," he says, "is that it isn't good for their physical development through the age of 14 and their intellectual development through the age of 16. I've seen some wasted kids, and it's really a sad situation." Many health officials and medical researchers — including several who appeared before the recent Senate Judiciary subcommittee hearings — have gone from a relaxed attitude toward pot to expressions of deep concern. Dr. DuPont put himself in that category during his testimony. Among other expert witnesses was Dr. William Pollin, director of N.I.D.A., who said he considers marijuana "a major and serious public health hazard."

Pot smoking carries many of the same dangers as cigarette smoking. Studies have shown, for example, that because of the practice of inhaling and holding marijuana smoke deep in the lungs, the smoking of five joints a week is the equivalent of smoking 16 cigarettes a day in terms of impaired lung function. And such figures do not take into consideration the use, particularly by younger smokers, of such paraphernalia as "power hitters" that shoot the smoke deep into the lungs.

But marijuana and its major psychoactive ingredient, delta 9 tetrahydrocannabinol, known as THC, are accused of evils beyond the precincts of tobacco. Definitive studies on human subjects are lacking, but the results of initial tests, on humans and on animals have clearly frightened parents. Rhesus monkeys, trained to smoke a joint five days a week for six months, a habit on the lower levels of heavy use, showed permanent changes in the structure of their brain cells. The body's immunological system, which fights infection, may be impaired by heavy pot smoking. The use of marijuana increases the heart rate up to 50 percent, making it perilous for those with or inclined toward heart ailments. And animal tests have shown that THC-treated females are four times more likely to abort or have stillborn young than untreated females.

The danger of heavy pot use for children of grammar-school and junior-high-school age is perceived to be greater than for adult smokers. One test, for example, that has many scientists concerned showed a reduction among adult pot smokers in the levels of testosterone, the hormone that controls the masculinizing process in pubescent boys. Another study showed a reduction in the sperm count in young adults as the use of marijuana increased.

There is another kind of hazard for young users that some parents find even more worrisome. Dr. Mitchell Rosenthal, president of Phoenix House Foundation, the nation's largest private drug-treatment program, puts it in these terms: "To grow, to develop, to achieve adulthood, adolescents must cope with the emotional storms and squalls of the troubled teen-age period. If they turn to marijuana, they establish a pattern of escaping rather than dealing with reality. They do not learn how to cope."

Among the psychological effects of heavy pot use cited by teachers and parents are a loss of interest in schoolwork, a tendency to lie without any feelings of guilt ("She stared me straight in the face," one mother said of her junior-high-school daughter, "tears running down her cheeks, swearing she was telling the truth about something, and I knew she was lying") and a change in attitude toward the family. "I realized," said a woman of her 12- year-old, "that right under our noses our happy, lovely little girl had turned into a sullen, alienated, unreasonable creature." Dr. Harold Voth, staff psychiatrist at the Menninger Foundation in Topeka, Kan., echoes that thought: "Marijuana is the great alienator."

But as many experts point out, not all the problems of the younger generation can be laid at marijuana's door. Larry Schott, national director of the National Organization for the Reform of Marijuana Laws (NORML), insists that the problems of many smokers predate their use of the drug. "Alcohol or marijuana or whatever," he says, "is going to be a crutch or it may aggravate the situation or kick off a situation that may be latent. But the problems lead to the substance and not the other way around."

Another factor that may have spurred the formation of parents' groups has been the nation's economic problems. As Robert Petersen of NIDA points out, "People do get more cautious as things get tougher economically." And though parents themselves have not made an issue of it, Kevin McEneaney of Phoenix House feels certain that there is concern about children's prospects in that kind of climate. "Parents are acutely aware," he says, "that the competition for jobs and education is going to be very, very tough."

IN THE SPRING of 1978, Pat and Bill Barton of Naples, Fla., discovered that their 17-year-old son and 15-year-old daughter were heavy marijuana users. The boy had been in a number of auto accidents and had disciplinary problems in school; the girl was dating a dope dealer. They sought professional counseling as a family, but they also called the parents of their children's best friends and suggested a get-together to discuss drugs.

These 10 men and women — what is known in the field as a parents' peer group — became the nucleus for the 500-member Naples Informed Parents Group, whose program is a model for such organizations around the nation. NIP, as it is known, successfully pushed for the passage of ordinances to outlaw head shops and other paraphernalia outlets. It persuaded local television and radio stations to carry public-service announcements about pot, established reference libraries on marijuana in the public schools and got the local medical society to include the subject in its "health awareness" program in the grammar schools. Monthly meetings are open to the public.

Much of the focus has been on Naples High School. At the group's urging, local sheriffs staked out the 1,500-student school for three weeks; they photographed 200 youngsters involved with drugs, and they arrested about a dozen. A tough new code of conduct for the school was developed that forbids paraphernalia or any controlled substances without prescription and gives school officials the right to search students. Streets leading to the school have been blocked off, and any person on the grounds who is not connected with the school and has not registered with the principal's office may be arrested. A volunteer group of mothers has been organized to check in with the parents of any children absent from school.

A special assistant principal was hired to help enforce these provisions. Punishments are steep. For a first offense for possession of paraphernalia, for example, the student faces possible suspension with referral of the case to police.

In general, though, the schools have done little to impede the spread of pot smoking in their precincts. One law-enforcement official says that, with few exceptions, most school administrators he has met "blame everybody but themselves. They aren't doing their jobs, and they refuse to own up to the problem."

In the last year, though, the numbers of those exceptions have been growing. Gregory R. Anrig, Massachusetts Commissioner of Education, says he's seeing "more severe suspensions that are drug-related." Police have been asked by some New England schools to film students between or after classes; typically, the parents of students observed to be dealing or smoking are invited to school to see the film and talk with administrators about correcting the problem. At Roosevelt Junior

High School in West Orange, N.J., Principal Murray Brooks tells of an intensified effort against drugs. Among the new approaches: "We have teachers on 'potty patrol' — they watch the bathrooms constantly during the day."

One of the most dramatic public responses to the spread of pot was initiated by New Jersey school administrators who appealed for help to the Essex County Bureau of Narcotics and Controlled Dangerous Substances. A special grand jury was convened. Undercover agents were placed in county schools and photographers set up outside the schools. More than a hundred witnesses, including students and parents, paraded before the grand jury, which issued its report last March.

"Marijuana use among our young," the report said, "may be the most dangerous situation we have faced as a nation in many years." The report spoke of 8-year-olds smoking pot and dealing, of a dramatic increase in smoking, making its use "open, notorious and pervasive."

Since the report was issued, schools in the county have brought in drug specialists to speak to students and teachers; drug-monitoring programs have been set up. Legislation has been introduced in the legislature in Trenton that would require drug education starting in kindergarten. Indications are that drug use in the county schools has diminished, and another grand-jury investigation is scheduled for next spring. But Richard Roberts, director of the Essex County bureau, is not impressed. He says the same quantity of pot is smoked by schoolchildren, but more of it is now smoked away from the schools.

SHE RUNS HER OWN business in Burlington, Wis., a tiny town some 30 miles south of Milwaukee. Her husband is a white-collar worker in a local factory. Their two sons are 12 and 13 years of age.

"My boys started smoking pot about a year ago," she says. "I only found out when they started skipping school. My oldest changed completely — started having tantrums, flying off the handle. The whole town is filled with parents like me. Their kids are stoned, some as young as third grade. But they're sitting back and having nervous breakdowns about it.

"The school says its hands are tied. The police department, they told me that I should not jeopardize my home, my business, my husband's job. But I saw one of my kids stoned. He was happy, smiling, acting like he really enjoyed it. That's when I knew I had to get this town together and start doing something."

Peggy Bruce (a pseudonym) has written to parents' organizations around the country for advice and materials to help her get a group started in Burlington. She exemplifies what Texas entrepreneur H. Ross Perot calls "the strongest human instinct I have observed." Mr. Perot has been appointed by the Governor to head a commission called Texans' War on Drugs. "I don't care whether it's a mamma bear or a mamma cat or a good American mother in an American town," says Mr. Perot. "When she feels her young are threatened in any way, she becomes a very powerful force."

Lee Dogoloff, associate director for drug policy at the White House, echoes those sentiments. "The parents," he says, "have been extremely influential in terms of the effect they have had on Government policy." On the Federal level, that has included a greatly accelerated campaign against marijuana. The National Institute on Drug Abuse, for example, has produced a new 30-minute educational film on marijuana, primarily for adults, and is making 400 copies available free of charge to parents' groups and schools; it is developing a new fact book advising parents how to deal with their children's pot problems and has just brought out another book describing the evolution of a pioneer group, Families in Action, in DeKalb County, Ga.

The Federal Government has also just made available to state and local governments a model law to help them crack down on head shops and other purveyors of rolling paper and paraphernalia. As commercial ventures, paraphernalia outlets are a most vulnerable facet of the drug culture and favorite targets of parents' groups. But some civil-liberties groups have opposed particular laws to outlaw paraphernalia on constitutional grounds, and there is no uniformity in state laws on the subject. It was this confusion that led the Government to offer its model law, covering "all equipment, products and materials of any kind which are used in ... ingesting, inhaling or otherwise introducing into the human body a controlled substance in violation of this act" — that is, a controlled substance as defined by the state law to which the model law would be attached.

Those in the antidrug field — Robert Kramer, for example, the Anne Arundel County drug-abuse expert — insist that the exotic gadgets that are now part of the paraphernalia scene are aimed at and purchased by the very young smoker, and are often more significant in getting him to start using pot than the experience of smoking itself.

The products include the likes of "grass masks," which look like gas masks except that the tube under the chin goes to a pipe instead of an oxygen tank, and baby bottles, complete with a bowl for the pot on the side and a rubber nipple through which to draw the smoke. Kevin McEneaney, an executive at Phoenix House, says, "You won't find many of your adult smokers pulling these things out of their pockets. They're aimed at kids." Andy Kowal, the publisher of the paraphernalia trade magazine, insists that they are bought, as a joke, by smokers over 30 years of age. "A kid," he says, "doesn't want to smoke out of a baby bottle — he's trying to get away from the bottle, not back to it."

Paraphernalia sales, nationwide, are estimated at upward of $350 million a year. Twelve states have passed laws against the gadgets, as have hundreds of communities in 43 states. On Long Island, for instance, Floral Park, Massapequa and Oyster Bay are among the communities that have taken steps to remove head shops. Lawrence and Cedarhurst passed ordinances last year after the opening of a head shop called Cosmik Debris, specializing in crystal bongs and gold-plated pipes selling for hundreds of dollars. Thus far, though, there's no indication that such moves have made major inroads on national sales figures.

PARENTS AND OTHER ADULTS who have sought to combat teen-age marijuana smoking have often found themselves running a gantlet of criticism. Many adults who smoke occasionally consider such efforts naive and exaggerated. Teenagers take a similar stance. "At first," said a woman in Florida, "we allowed ourselves as parents to be bullied into thinking that if we made a fuss about marijuana, we were out of it." Sometimes the opposition takes an ugly form.

Joe and Wilma Frayne — not their real names — and their three children live in upstate New York, where he teaches at a community college. About a year ago, they began noticing the smell of pot on their 13-year-old daughter's clothes; then they found a plastic bag of grass on the kitchen floor, and traced it to their older son, who was 16; finally, they learned that their 12-year-old had also been turned on to grass.

The Fraynes talked to other families in the neighborhood, trying to organize a parents' peer group, but the adults refused to acknowledge that their own children might be involved with drugs. The neighborhood children felt the Fraynes and their youngsters had "narced" on them, played the informer. The family's house and car have been pelted with eggs; teen-agers drive by and toss bottles into the yard and shout obscenities. Joe and Wilma are looking forward to the end of the college year; they are going to move.

The couple is totally discouraged, and they don't even know just what they would have done differently to prevent their children from becoming potheads. "It seemed out of our control," Wilma says, "as though we had no power over it. Movies, rock music, magazines. Even if you locked them in the house, they'd still get all those drug messages."

Others are similarly disheartened. Says Barry Wilansky, director of the TEMPO drug-rehabilitation program on Long Island, "In the 60's, one smoked listening to Dylan and the Beatles and songs about peace and love and justice. In the 70's, pot is associated with rock and disco madness and aggressiveness. The media make Studio 54 and its drug behavior glamorous."

Dr. Nicholas Pace, a professor at New York University Medical Center, speaks of "a whole generation going down the tube," and asks, in a tone that suggests he knows the answer, "Are we going to see a nation of drones?" Dr. Ingrid Lantner, an Ohio pediatrician, fears that nothing will be done "until we taxpayers are forced to pay higher taxes to support these people when they get out of school and can't even hold a job."

A 15-year-old junior at Woodmere Academy on Long Island, who has come down off a habit of eight to 10 "J's" a day, offered a measure of optimism. "I don't know what the scene will be by the time we grow up and have kids," she said, "but it cannot be the same as it is now. It's just gotten too outrageous."

ELISABETH COLEMAN BRYNNER is a freelance writer based in Pawling, N.Y.

Marijuana as Medicine

EDITORIAL | BY THE NEW YORK TIMES | AUG. 27, 1983

SMOKING MARIJUANA may be harmful to your health, doctors warn. But they also know that in the case of several illnesses, marijuana is the therapeutic drug of choice. It reduces nausea for patients undergoing cancer treatment, for instance, and arrests developing blindness in glaucoma victims.

Because of this medical value of marijuana, 31 states have approved its use under competent supervision. But Washington controls the supply of both marijuana and Delta-9-THC, a synthetic derivative. And thus far, the Federal bureaucracy has been unconscionably slow to provide the materials for medical therapy. Representative Stewart McKinney of Connecticut and 51 co-sponsors in the House deserve support for their bill to streamline the supply process.

Relatively little is known about the chemically complex marijuana plant. But the National Academy of Sciences finds that it may have medical uses ranging from the treatment of epilepsy to asthma to anorexia. And it has powerful, proven value both in reducing the wrenching nausea caused by anti-cancer drugs and in controlling glaucoma, the leading cause of blindness.

Horror stories of mothers having to buy marijuana illegally for 5-year-olds with leukemia have persuaded most state legislatures to loosen their drug laws. But as far as the Feds are concerned, pot remains a "Schedule I" drug under the Controlled Substances Act, which means it is available only for experimentation and only under the most rigid controls. Physicians naturally balk at the tedious, hypocritical procedure for obtaining "experimental" substances that everyone knows are for non-experimental purposes. As a result, patients who know their way around buy marijuana, of uncertain purity, on the street. Those who are not streetwise must do without. Mr. McKinney's bill would not make pot available at the supermarket. It would not even permit physicians to prescribe marijuana as freely as they now dole out dangerous amphetamines, barbiturates and opiates. But it would recognize marijuana as medically useful and set up simple procedures for responsible doctors and hospitals to obtain it. This measure offers Congress a sensible way to relieve suffering and remedy illness. There's every reason to do both, and quickly.

Anti-Drug Law: Words, Deeds, Political Expediency

BY JOEL BRINKLEY | OCT. 27, 1986

AS PRESIDENT REAGAN formally opened the White House's campaign against drug abuse in early August, he articulated a notion that has been growing among drug law-enforcement officials over the last few years.

It is that law enforcement cannot significantly reduce drug abuse. The real answer to the nation's drug problem, Mr. Reagan asserted repeatedly through the late summer and early fall, was a "national crusade" to educate people not to use drugs.

Still, on Monday, when Mr. Reagan plans to sign the most far-reaching drug law ever passed by Congress, the Anti-Drug Abuse Act of 1986, only a handful of its several dozen new programs and provisions will be spent for drug education. Just 12 percent of the $1.7 billion in financing will be spent for that purpose. Most of the rest will go for new boats, planes and weapons, more drug law-enforcement agents, added Federal prosecutors and new jail cells.

In his speech at the White House Aug. 4, Mr. Reagan said, "We've waged a good fight," but he added: "Drug use continues and its consequences escalate. All the confiscation and law enforcement in the world will not cure this plague."

EMPHASIS ON EDUCATION

Many members of Congress and drug law-enforcement officials heartily agreed. For example, at a news conference Friday, called to urge the television networks to provide more anti-drug programming, Representative Charles E. Schumer, a Brooklyn Democrat, said: "The drug boom is fueled by the demand of our children. We need to educate our young people to the hazards of drug abuse. Focusing on the supply side alone won't solve the drug problem."

But the new drug bill does not seem to reflect that view.

One reason it is so heavily weighted toward enforcement, said John T. Cusack, chief of staff for the House Select Committee on Narcotics Abuse and Control, is that law enforcement is more expensive; a dollar spent in a classroom buys more than a dollar given to drug law-enforcement agencies.

But a larger reason is that drug education is not politically expedient. The drug bill authorizes about $200 million to be given to the states for a variety of school and community education programs. It also establishes several new Government agencies and commissions to coordinate a national drug education campaign.

DELAY IN SEEING RESULTS

But experts in the field say none of that will produce noticeable results this year or next. Drug education may not produce many noticeable effects for a generation, long after most of the Government officials and members of Congress who crafted this bill will have left office.

At the same time, the $1.1 billion in the bill dedicated to local state and Federal law-enforcement agencies is likely to produce immediate, visible results: bags of cocaine seized, drug traffickers sent to jail.

To that end, the drug bill authorizes nearly $300 million for strengthened drug law-enforcement on the Mexican border, including money for radar balloons, airplanes, helicopters and boats. It establishes a $10 million drug law-enforcement task force in the Bahamas. It gives the states $230 million for enhancing local enforcement capabilities. It nearly doubles the State Department's $60 million budget for drug law-enforcement abroad.

The bill increases fines and prison terms for drug offenses tenfold or more, in some cases. To deal with all the new inmates, it authorizes $96.5 million for new Federal prisons and orders the Department of Defense to see if it has any spare buildings that can be converted to jails.

No one in the enforcement agencies is unhappy to get the hundreds of millions of dollars in additional money, but some officials note that they are not entirely sure what to do with it.

For example, shortly after the White House announced that it would spend $100 million for a new drug interdiction program along the Gulf Coast, the heads of Federal enforcement agencies, who were meeting in September, all realized that the money had not been allotted to any specific agency yet.

SUDDENLY, A 'LOOSE' BASKETBALL

"Suddenly it was like a basketball had popped loose, and everyone was all over the floor trying to grab it," a senior drug law-enforcement official said. Each of the agencies was asked to draft a plan for spending the money.

Although enforcement officials are increasingly open about the conclusion that enforcing the law is not the answer to drug abuse, some of the drafters of the drug bill say enforcement has failed only because it has received inadequate financing.

"We've never really tried it," Representative Glenn English, an Oklahoma Democrat who sponsored significant portions of the new drug bill, said recently. "Our people have always been hopelessly outmanned and outgunned by the traffickers."

A House aide who wrote much of the bill said, "Now for the first time we are going to give the traffickers a fight on near-even terms."

The bill also allots more money for treatment of current drug abusers and for drug research, about $375 million, than it does for drug education.

Mr. Cusack, whose committee had a major hand in drafting significant portions of the drug bill, acknowledged that at $200 million, financing for education programs was dwarfed by the money for enforcement and other programs. But previously, he said, the Federal Government spent almost nothing on drug education. Last year, $23 million was spent for that purpose.

"In many ways it's very simple to increase and expand programs that have been in existence for a long time," Mr. Cusack said. "But in many places these education programs don't even exist."

Bush, Citing Cost, Says Drug War Will Focus Largely on Education

BY GERALD M. BOYD | JAN. 26, 1989

PRESIDENT BUSH said today that the all-out war on drugs he promised in his Inaugural Address would be mainly an educational effort rather than a law-enforcement crackdown.

Mr. Bush said he was taking the educational approach because the "overriding problem of the deficit" would make it difficult to increase spending on border patrols and other efforts to keep drugs out of the country.

The new President's remarks suggested that he agreed with those who have argued that the only long-term solution lies in curbing the demand for illegal drugs.

SUPPLY VS. DEMAND

In the Inaugural Address, he said flatly, "This scourge will stop." Asked to elaborate on that statement today, he said:

"The answer to the problem of drugs lies more on solving the demand side of the equation than it does on the supply side, than it does on interdiction or sealing the borders or something of that nature. And so it is going to have to be a major educational effort, and the private sector and the schools are all going to have to be involved in this."

Mr. Bush's comments came in a 12-minute interview with two reporters in the Oval Office. It was the first under a new White House plan to make him more accessible to the press than President Reagan was. The President touched on a number of topics, including the prospect of a visit to China next month. And he strongly backed Dr. Louis W. Sullivan, his choice for Secretary of Health and Human Services, whose position on abortion has caused concern among conservatives. Though aides said Mr. Bush had no plans to reverse the Reagan Administration's decision to attend the human rights conference in Moscow in 1991, the President said he would evaluate the Soviet commitment to human rights over the next two years before the planned meeting.

"I think that we need to look for performance," Mr. Bush said. "And there will be time in which to see performance in that regard." Referring to testimony last week by James A. Baker 3d, his nominee for Secretary of State, he added, "And I think the Soviets know that we feel this way."

CHINA VISIT UNDER STUDY

The President said there had been "definite improvement in some ways" in human rights in the Soviet Union. "But let's see what develops as we move towards that conference day."

Mr. Bush also suggested that he was considering a visit to China, where he served as chief of liaison for the United States mission in 1974. "Stay tuned," he said. The stop would be added to the President's itinerary when he travels to Japan late next month for the funeral of Emperor Hirohito.

Brent Scowcroft, the national security adviser, has been trying to make final plans for the visit, which was first reported this week by the Yugoslav press agency, Tanyug.

Mr. Bush said he did not know yet if he would seek an increase in Federal spending to combat illegal drugs.

"We have got to use this office to encourage all elements of our society to participate in the fight against drugs, in the fight to improve education or working to make the environment better, because we are dealing with scarce resources in terms of Federal money," he said.

Critics in Congress today questioned the new President's commitment to the campaign against drugs, pointing out that he had not included William J. Bennett, the head of the Administration's anti-drug effort, in the first meeting of the Cabinet.

Congress created the position of director of national drug control policy last year, hoping to coordinate the Government's anti-drug efforts. The director receives the same pay as Cabinet members and must be confirmed by the Senate, but the President can decide whether or not to make him a participating member of the Cabinet.

"We were not talking about standing at the door when we created the title of drug czar," said Representative Charles B. Rangel, Democrat of New York and chairman of the Select Committee on Narcotics Abuse and Control. "And nothing short of full participation is expected by the House and Senate." He added that there could be "a serious confrontation with Congress" if Mr. Bush refused to alter his decision.

A Republican member of the select committee, Representative Robert K. Dornan of California, said, "The President will have to rethink this if this is really going to stay at the war level everyone wants it to be."

BENNETT'S UNCERTAIN STATUS

In the Senate, Alan J. Dixon, Democrat of Illinois, today introduced a bill that would make Mr. Bennett a Cabinet member.

White House officials said Mr. Bennett's lack of Cabinet rank would not diminish his authority, and added that he may still be invited to some Cabinet sessions. John P. Walters, an aide to Mr. Bennett, said Mr. Bush's decision "doesn't in my view reflect any lack of commitment by President Bush to Mr. Bennett or any doubt about the President's seriousness on the drug initiative."

Later today, Mr. Bush signed an executive order establishing an eight-member Presidential commission of attorneys and former Government officials to recommend ways to strengthen the laws governing the ethical conduct of members of Congress and senior Administration officials. The head of the bipartisan panel will be Malcolm R. Wilkey Jr., a former senior judge on the United States Court of Appeals for the District of Columbia. The vice chairman will be Griffin B. Bell, who was Attorney General in the Carter Administration.

'AN UNAMBIGUOUS CODE'

Mr. Bush has been saying this week that high ethical standards would be a priority in his Administration. His aides have denied that the statements are part of an effort to contrast his Administration with Mr. Reagan's, in which numerous high-ranking officials were accused of ethical lapses.

"We need an unambiguous code," Mr. Bush said, "a code of conduct, to insure that those who serve the public trust avoid any actual or apparent conflict between their personal and public interest." He called the current ethics statutes fragmented and confusing.

The commission is to make recommendations by March 9.

The new President is expected to underscore his concern about ethics in remarks Thursday to some 3,000 senior Government executives. Mr. Bush will stress the need to follow the precise provisions of ethics laws and to tell the officials "what he expects of them," said Marlin Fitzwater, the chief White House spokesman.

In today's interview, Mr. Bush left open the possibility of allowing oil drilling in the Arctic National Wildlife Refuge in Alaska. This was recommended by the Interior Department in the last days of the Reagan Administration, prompting expressions of concern from more than 100 civic and environmental groups.

'I REMEMBER THE PIPELINE'

Mr. Bush said that while he was "determined to be an environmentalist," he was not certain that such drilling should be prohibited.

"I'm in favor of prudent development there," he said.

"I remember the pipeline," he added, recalling another battle over Alaskan oil in the early 1970's. "I remember the arguments against it. And I also know the effect it did not have on the caribou."

The new President has not said how he will proceed on the budget and other issues. Asked if he was setting too deliberate a pace, he said he thought it was "a little early to make conclusions, one way or another, on all that."

The High Hidden Costs of the War on Marijuana

BY PETER PASSELL | SEPT. 5, 1989

COCAINE IS NOT the only losing front in the Government's war on drugs. In what experts regard as the most authoritative study of the illegal market for marijuana, a Harvard economist has concluded that the billion-dollar Federal effort to disrupt the trade is a failure.

Tighter controls at the borders in the Reagan years did indeed reduce imports of marijuana, says the economist, Mark A. R. Kleiman of Harvard's Kennedy School of Government. But he argues that this merely stimulated domestic cultivation and encouraged producers and sellers to put far more potent forms of the drug on the market.

By cutting back on enforcement, Mr. Kleiman argues, the Government could reverse these two unintended effects and thereby advance the goals of anti-drug policy. Total consumption of delta-9-tetrahydrocannabinol or THC, the active ingredient in marijuana, would probably fall, he says. So would the profits of drug traffickers.

'COSTS OF CONTROL'

It is not clear how these conclusions, in Mr. Kleiman's new book, "Marijuana: Costs of Abuse, Costs of Control" (Greenwood Press), will be received in Washington.

There seems to be little sentiment, either in Washington or among the general public, for treating marijuana differently from illegal drugs like cocaine and heroin. On the other hand, Mr. Kleiman's call for a relaxation of the effort to stop marijuana imports may mesh with the Bush Administration's general inclination to spend more of its anti-drug budget on prosecution of drug offenders and treatment of users. President Bush is scheduled to present the Administration's anti-drug strategy in a broadcast speech tonight.

The Federal war on marijuana, Mr. Kleiman says, has been anchored by the simple idea that one ton confiscated by the Customs Service or the Drug Enforcement Administration is one ton less consumed. In this case, he believes, simplicity is misleading.

Confiscated marijuana has been replaced at low cost, he says, so the enforcement effort has had little effect on consumption. Moreover, as a closer look at the marijuana market suggests, the border crackdown has given rise to a much more potent form of the drug.

In the Carter years, Washington's limited effort to disrupt drug imports focused on cocaine and heroin. The Reagan Administration radically altered course, sharply increasing total expenditures on border controls and ending the unofficial policy of ignoring small shipments of marijuana.

The intensified search for marijuana, Mr. Kleiman reports, reduced imports from about 4,200 tons in 1982 to 3,900 in 1986. The price of the drug went up, compensating shippers and dealers for the added risk of property confiscation and arrest. Adjusted for inflation, the average retail price rose 35 percent, to about $84 an ounce.

STILL WIDELY AVAILABLE

Marijuana remains widely available, however, and a dollar still buys enough to get high. And the success in reducing imports has masked the ominous ways in which the market has adjusted.

The increased cost of importing marijuana stimulated domestic production, which rose 10 percent from 1982 to 1986, by Government estimates. And this infant industry of the 1970's has grown into a healthy giant: one-quarter of the marijuana sold in the United States is now home-grown. As Peter Reuter, an economist at the Rand Corporation, wryly pointed out, "This is the rare instance in which trade protectionism really worked."

Small-scale domestic producers, lacking farmland they can easily conceal, have had an incentive to cultivate sinsemilla, the sticky, seedless marijuana with a much higher content of the active ingredient,

THC, than ordinary marijuana. And with the help of cloning technology, says John P. Sutton of the Drug Enforcement Administration, Americans now grow "the most potent marijuana in the world." As a result, Mr. Kleiman estimates, the total amount of THC consumed by Americans actually rose 22 percent from 1982 to 1986.

The social cost, many experts believe, has similarly climbed. In the 1970's, marijuana sold in the United States had a THC content of 1 to 2 percent. Last year the D.E.A. confiscated marijuana whose THC content was as high as 18 percent. Smokers looking for the equivalent of a beer may thus unwittingly end up with a triple martini, with unfortunate consequences for job productivity.

HIGHER PROFITS THAN EVER

Another unwelcome effect of the Reagan policy, Mr. Kleiman argues, is on the way the marijuana market is organized. Tougher border controls, he believes, increased risks to all importers and drove poorly capitalized ones out of business. But the added costs to large, well-organized shippers, who could afford to lose an occasional boatload, were more than offset by the higher prices they could charge. The profits to those still in the trade, he concludes, are higher than ever.

One way to undo the unintended effects of the crackdown on marijuana, Mr. Kleiman says, would be to legalize it and regulate its purity and potency. Legal marijuana could be a major source of tax revenue rather than a $14 billion business for criminals and a billion-dollar cost to the Treasury. But there is little support for such a radical experiment; it is generally agreed that more people would smoke marijuana if it were legal, just as many more people began drinking alcohol with the end of Prohibition in 1933.

THE MIDDLE GROUND

Still, Mr. Kleiman argues, there may be a politically acceptable middle ground.

Cutting the Federal enforcement budget in half might increase consumption of marijuana by a few percent, he says, but it would probably reverse the changes in the market that have made marijuana much more potent and profitable in the 1980's. And lowering its potency would reduce the threat it poses to health, safety and productivity.

Some economic analysts take issue with some of Mr. Kleiman's findings. Mark Moore, also at the Kennedy School, says loosening border controls on marijuana would not save much money, since the same personnel would still be involved in the effort to block cocaine and heroin. But there is little disagreement among economists that the consequences of marijuana interdiction have been largely perverse.

Yet it may be hard to persuade policymakers and the public to treat marijuana differently from other drugs. Mathea Falco, an Assistant Secretary of State for narcotics matters in the Carter Administration who wrote a study on drugs for the Twentieth Century Fund, a research group in New York, points to a paradox in the evolution of drug policies.

PUBLIC MAKES FEW DISTINCTIONS

In the past decade, she says, the public has become much less willing to consider each drug as a separate problem, requiring a separate containment strategy, even though the social and medical consequences of the various drugs have been diverging widely. Cocaine, for example, used to be mainly a pleasure drug for the well-off; now crack, its cheap and smokable form, has run rampant through the inner cities, destroying families and neighborhoods. Heroin's destructiveness, too, has taken on a new dimension; addicts who share needles have become a major conduit for the spread of AIDS.

The Reagan Administration catered to the attitude that all drugs are unacceptable with its policy of "zero tolerance," the absolute prohibition of all illegal drugs. And the strategy paper released by William J. Bennett, the Bush Administration's director of drug control policy, makes few distinctions among illegal drugs or strategies for combating them.

But there is still one reason to believe that the Administration may quietly choose to deemphasize border control for drugs in general and marijuana in particular: money.

Attacking drug supply and demand at every level, as Mr. Bennett seems to be advocating, will be very expensive. And in the search for Federal cash to augment both law enforcement and drug treatment, it will be very tempting to tap the billion dollars a year that serve to protect domestic marijuana producers from foreign competition.

Booming Business: Drug Use Tests

BY MILT FREUDENHEIM | JAN. 3, 1990

AS EMPLOYERS BEGIN testing millions of transportation workers for drug use under Federal rules that took effect in December, the laboratories that conduct the tests say their business is surging.

But while industry executives and analysts expect the market to grow rapidly for at least a year or two, there are big uncertainties. For one thing, the legality of the testing has been challenged by unions. And the profitability of the procedure for commercial laboratories could come under pressure as competition heats up and prices are cut.

Five companies took in an estimated $173 million from testing for illegal drugs last year, or 75 percent of the market of $230 million, executives and industry analysts estimated. They are the SmithKline Beecham Company; Hoffmann-La Roche; Metpath, a unit of Corning; Compuchem, and Damon.

Revenues from testing for drug abuse will jump to $340 million this year, up 48 percent from 1989, these people estimated. All told, testing for illegal drugs accounted for less than 5 percent of the $5 billion in 1988 revenues of the 5,600 independent commercial laboratories, said Michael B. McNulty, vice president for corporate testing programs at the Clinical Laboratories unit of SmithKline.

The laboratories charge $30 to $35 a person, on average, for the stringently controlled screening and confirmation tests required under the Federal rules. That compares with $20 to $25 for drug testing of employees not subject to those rules.

But prices for the federally certified test could fall as new laboratories for the drug-testing program are approved by the Government. The National Institute on Drug Abuse has so far certified only 38 of the 500 laboratories that have applied to take part in the Federal program.

Four of the approved laboratories are owned by SmithKline and three by Hoffmann-La Roche.

"When all the good discounters come in, the price will come down to $20 per person," said Gerard A. Marini, president of Diagnostic Dimensions, a drug-testing unit of Hoffmann-La Roche Inc. and the fastest-growing company in the field.

Mr. Marini said some smaller laboratories had cut prices sharply, but he defended the higher prices as necessary to maintain quality. "Some people say they can get it done for $7," he said. But he added that if a client ordering a test at a cut-rate price from a fly-by-night laboratory was sued by an employee who contended that an error had been made, the laboratory might simply file for bankruptcy and leave the company responsible. "It has happened," he said.

While the lab profits are not noticeable on the bottom line at big, diversified companies like SmithKline and Hoffmann-La Roche, they are important to specialized labs like Compuchem, which said 60 percent of its business is in testing for illegal drugs.

While demand for the tests has been growing rapidly, the ultimate size of the market is uncertain. Unions representing truckers and other workers have filed lawsuits challenging the Federal rules on the ground that drug testing violates the constitutional prohibition of unwarranted searches.

"There are land mines everywhere in the business, undecided lawsuits to determine who can be tested and what the proper cause for testing might be," said Kenneth C. Bohringer, an analyst at Prudential-Bache Securities.

Under the new rules, four million transportation workers must eventually be tested, on a random basis. They include aviation employees, mass-transit workers, interstate bus and truck drivers, railroad workers and people in the marine and pipeline industries. Samples of their urine will be tested for five substances — marijuana, cocaine, opiates like heroin, amphetamines and the hallucinogenic tranquilizer phencyclidine, or PCP.

JOB APPLICANTS OFTEN TESTED

The transportation workers are joining 17 million Americans whose employers already have drug-testing programs. Most large companies test job applicants. Many test people in safety-sensitive positions or whose behavior raises suspicions. But only a handful of companies have conducted random testing of all employees.

Mr. McNulty at SmithKline said 8 million Americans were tested for illegal drugs last year. He estimated that 13 million would be tested in 1990 and 22 million in 1992.

To be certified for the tests, laboratories must meet tight requirements for accuracy, confidentiality and protection against tampering with results. Their workers must be federally accredited. When a preliminary screening test that picks up chemical reactions to a drug in a urine sample is positive, it must be confirmed with a new test of the same batch by an automated process called gas chromatography/mass spectrometry, which is supervised by a technician with a master's degree or doctorate.

A certifying scientist reviews the result and sends it to an authorized physician. The doctor, trying to make sure a mistake has not been made, interviews the person who was tested before reporting the results to the employer.

Laboratories that have one false positive test could be decertified, a spokeswoman at the Transportation Department said.

When all costs are considered, some employers might pay $60 to $85 a worker for services that include setting up the program and selecting the employees to be tested, said Dexter Morris, president of Drug Intervention Services of America. He said his company, based in Houston, has developed such programs for companies like Greyhound, Wal-Mart, Weyerhaeuser and Global Van Lines as well as several petrochemical companies.

Dr. Donald Ian Macdonald, who was a White House drug policy adviser in the Reagan Administration, listed some of the costs facing employers in the Federal program.

"A policy has to be written," he said. "That's money for lawyers. A minimum of one hour of training for supervisors is required: money for trainers. Urine is collected forensically: money for collectors. Samples are taken in a hurry to a certified laboratory: money for Federal Express. And tests are reviewed by a licensed physician and then reported to the company." Dr. Macdonald is president of Employee Health Programs, based in Washington, which provides physician reviewers.

LONG-TERM SAVINGS

The Transportation Department has estimated that the program will cost industry $2 billion over 10 years to administer, but will yield savings of $8.7 billion because of fewer accidents and lower rates of absenteeism and other drug-related problems.

Doctors in Survey Support Marijuana Use by Cancer Patients

BY JOSEPH B. TREASTER | MAY 1, 1990

NEARLY HALF of the cancer specialists responding to a questionnaire on the controversial subject of marijuana used as medicine said they would prescribe the drug if it were legal, researchers at Harvard University said yesterday.

A slightly smaller percentage of the specialists answering the mailed questionnaire said that despite the illegality of the drug they had already recommended it to patients as a way of finding relief from nausea resulting from chemotherapy and for enhancing appetite.

"This clearly shows that a large percentage of cancer specialists believe that marijuana can be beneficial to their patients," said Richard Doblin, one of the researchers.

For the survey, which is to be summarized in Wednesday's issue of the Annals of Internal Medicine, the researchers sent questionnaires to 2,430 members of the American Society of Clinical Oncology and received 1,035 responses.

A full report of the survey is to be published in the Sept. 1 issue of the Journal of Clinical Oncology, the society's official journal. The survey was not an official Harvard study, the researchers said.

RANDOMLY SELECTED

The researchers said they randomly selected members of the society from around the country. Dr. Joseph Bailes, the chairman of the society's clinical practice committee, said the organization has about 8,500 members.

Advocates of marijuana, the most widely used illegal drug in the United States, have been struggling in the courts for nearly 20 years to have it reclassified under the Federal Controlled Substances Act so that it can be sold under prescription. But the Federal Drug

Enforcement Administration, which is charged with establishing controls over drugs in this country, argues that marijuana has no clear medical value and insists that it continue to be classified among the most dangerous drugs, including heroin and LSD.

A synthetic form of marijuana has been available in tablet form by prescription since 1985. But Mr. Doblin and Mark A. R. Kleiman, drug specialists at the John F. Kennedy School of Government at Harvard, said that cancer specialists responding to their survey considered smoked marijuana to be more effective and "roughly as safe."

Dr. Bailes, a cancer specialist in McAllen, Tex., said he was not aware of any data to support the proposition that "smoking works better."

MEDICAL USES

Marijuana has also been used to treat glaucoma, neurological disorders and, recently, to relieve nausea and enhance appetite in AIDS patients, according to Government health officials. The Federal Government has issued exceptions permitting about two dozen people to legally use marijuana for medical problems, mainly cancer, a spokesman for the Food and Drug Administration said.

One of the guiding standards for the Drug Enforcement Agency in classifying drugs is whether there is a "currently accepted medical use in treatment in the United States."

Three years ago, Francis Young, the Administrative Judge of the Drug Enforcement Administration declared that marijuana "in its natural form, is one of the safest therapeutically active substances known to man," and he recommended that physicians be authorized to prescribe it. But the chief of the agency then, John C. Lawn, refused to relax the restrictions. Last week, a Federal appeals court sent the case back to the drug agency for clarification of its position.

Kevin B. Zeese, an official of the Drug Policy Foundation, an independent research center in Washington, who has been acting as chief counsel to the National Organization for the Reform of Marijuana

Laws, said the findings were "consistent with what we saw as we presented evidence before the DEA between 1986 and 1988."

"We had testimony from every region of the country indicating that doctors were aware of their patients' use of marijuana as medicine and, in many cases, they encouraged it," Mr. Zeese said.

Dr. Bailes said he had "no opinion on whether this survey would represent the thinking of our whole membership or not," adding, "We have never polled our members." He said he thought the medical use of marijuana was becoming "considerably less of an issue" because "a lot of new anti-nausea agents are becoming available."

The Drug Enforcement Administration chose not to comment on the decision by the appeals court or on the Harvard survey.

Scientists Learn How Marijuana Works in Brain

BY PHILIP J. HILTS | JULY 21, 1990

RESEARCHERS PLAN TO report that they have discovered receptors in the brain that are stimulated by marijuana, suggesting that the body produces a substance similar to marijuana and uses it to relieve pain and stress.

The discovery of the chemical mechanism suggests that researchers might eventually be able to develop drugs that do not cause intoxication but have some of the medicinal properties of marijuana, including relief of pain, asthma, nausea and convulsions.

Researchers might also be able to design new types of drugs aimed at these receptors that are more effective pain killers.

"This opens up a whole new system in the body," said Dr. Louis Harris, chairman of pharmacology and toxicology at the Medical College of Virginia, whose laboratories have worked on the problem.

A receptor is a molecule on a cell surface that acts like a keyhole to receive a key in the form of a hormone, drug or other substance that, when locked on the cell, creates a change in the body. The discovery of such a molecule occurring naturally in the body means that the body makes a substance like marijuana.

EARLIER FINDINGS ON OPIATES

A similar discovery two decades ago opened up much of the current work on receptors, when Dr. Solomon Snyder, a Johns Hopkins University neuroscientist, and his colleagues located the receptor where heroin, morphine and other opiates act. It was later found that there were "natural opiates," called enkephalins, which the body produces and uses to relieve pain and stress.

Natural substances that have such powerful action have enormous potential, said Dr. Julius Axelrod, a chemist from the National

Institutes of Health. He said the natural substances could be used to make more effective drugs.

"This is a very exciting finding," said Dr. Axelrod, who predicted that many laboratories would begin a search for the "natural marijuana" that the body produces.

The discovery was reported Wednesday at a meeting at the National Academy of Sciences' Institute of Medicine, which designated the 1990's the "Decade of the Brain."

A UNIQUE PAIN RELIEVER

Dr. Snyder reported that Dr. Michael Brownstein, chief of the laboratory of cell biology at the National Institute of Mental Health, had discovered the receptor. Dr. Brownstein, who has worked with Dr. Snyder in previous research, declined to discuss the new work, which he has submitted for publication in the British journal Nature.

Dr. Snyder said the discovery opens up research into another natural chemical pathway for relieving pain.

Dr. Billy R. Martin of the Medical College of Virginia, who has worked for years to find a marijuana-derived pain reliever without the drug's side effects, said the compounds were unique. He said a drug based on the body's form of marijuana would use a completely different pain killing mechanism from that of the natural opiates.

"We have been waiting for this for years," said Dr. Martin.

'NOT JUST AN ACCIDENT'

The body uses an array of hormones, neurotransmitters and other chemicals to trigger effects, like the reactions that come with anger, or to regulate the operation of different organs, like the regular beat of the heart. The chemicals the body uses to do this act by being released from one cell and binding to another.

In the case of the just-discovered receptor, one of the effects may be the release of a mild, natural painkiller.

"Humans or animals didn't evolve a receptor for some chemical out of a plant," said Dr. Harris, "and it's not just an accident that they fit. The body makes these receptors to accept chemicals that are important."

The "natural marijuana" receptor has been found primarily in the regions of the brain where higher mental activity takes place. Other major psychotropic drugs like heroin, amphetamines, and cocaine affect lower brain activities, like heartbeat and respiration, in dangerous ways.

LOW DOSES ARE EFFECTIVE

Marijuana's active ingredient, tetrahydrocannabinol, or THC, has a number of effects that interest researchers. It creates effects at doses that are very low compared to the doses at which life-threatening complications might occur.

In addition to causing euphoria and a number of other psyhcological effects, it can be used to retard glaucoma, to treat asthma, to stop seizures, to lower blood pressure and other effects.

Marijuana's most harmful effects come not from the substance itself, but from the inhaling of its smoke, which acts much like tobacco smoke. It has been suggested that other harmful effects, such as attention disorders, are caused by the drug, but the effects are not themselves considered very serious or irreversible.

Often, a drug's different effects are triggered by different subgroups of the main receptor, Dr. Snyder said, so discovery of the main receptor for marijuana would likely lead to a family of other receptors whose functions are somewhat different.

One thing that may be found is an antagonist that reverses the effect of THC. Researchers say it is not clear if the discovery would have much impact in drug treatment, however, because marijuana is not addictive and therefore little would be gained by blocking its action as methadone blocks the action of heroin.

Officials of the National Institute of Mental Health refused to discuss the research, saying that the editors of Nature had asked them not to discuss it before its scheduled publication in the next few weeks.

Costly and Scarce, Marijuana Is a High More Are Rejecting

BY JOSEPH B. TREASTER | OCT. 29, 1991

NOT LONG AGO, hosts at some Upper East Side dinner parties would set out little silver bowls of home-rolled marijuana cigarettes along with the after-dinner drinks. Rock concerts unfolded under canopies of marijuana smoke, and the drug's syrupy aroma drifted across schoolyards and campuses, construction sites and corporate offices, public parks and private patios.

But as quietly and gradually as the widening of a waistline, America's infatuation with the herb of many names — grass, pot, dope, weed, ganja, sess, sens, smoke, skunk and, quaintly, in the long ago, Mary Jane — has been fading.

In New York and throughout the country, lighting up is no longer hip, not in high school, not at college, not at most social events and, with the advent of widespread random drug testing, certainly not on the job.

'IT'S NOT COOL ANYMORE'

The great marijuana cloud has grown wispy as rebellion and the quest for nirvana have yielded to conformity and the struggle for survival, as health concerns and a vague fear of getting into trouble have risen above the desire to get giddy.

Part of the shift, undoubtedly, has also been because of relentless police pressure that has transformed an abundant drug once available for $20 or $30 an ounce into a scarce commodity selling in some quarters of New York for $800 an ounce, more than twice the price of gold.

"It's not cool anymore," said a high school senior in Manhattan, capturing the mood of the 90's with the language of the 60's.

Although the glory days of the Beatles are generally remembered as the peak of the marijuana craze, the popularity of the drug gathered momentum through the 70's and stayed relatively strong until the late 80's.

Advocates insist that marijuana — the mildest and by far the most widely tried illegal drug in America — is no more harmful than alcohol, not even the latest strains, which are 10 times more potent than the grass of the flower children. Still, it has been as much a target of the national antidrug campaign as cocaine, heroin, LSD and barbiturates, and many people have clearly taken the prohibitions to heart.

No conclusive medical evidence on the long-term effects of marijuana has been developed. But Federal officials contend it is a steppingstone to other drugs. Many addicts do report that marijuana was their first drug. But legions of former smokers say they never went on to anything stronger. "Most of us," said one professional woman in her mid-40's, "just dropped out of drugs and called it a day."

Ultimately, it seems, marijuana just does not fit the personal visions of growing numbers of New Yorkers and other Americans. Nor do most other drugs, including cocaine, alcohol and nicotine, all of which are being increasingly rejected.

Some of those most militantly opposed to marijuana and other drugs are schoolchildren who for several years now have been attending antidrug classes and watching antidrug messages on television. One junior high student in Queens said she had no interest in experimenting with marijuana. "It just doesn't seem like it would be fun or anything," she said. "We've heard so much about it, that it's horrible and stuff."

'USING POT IS LIKE DROPPING OUT'

And the Manhattan high school senior said that although marijuana was widely accepted as recently as her freshman and sophomore years, she now finds that "everyone is really scared about getting into college and getting good jobs and doing drugs doesn't help." The two young women, like many other people interviewed for this article, spoke on the condition that they not be identified because they were socially uncomfortable about being associated with drugs in any way.

"Using pot," the high school senior said, "is like dropping out of the race"; which, of course, was precisely the attraction for many in her father's generation.

Former pot smokers — or almost-former pot smokers — are everywhere. Nathan J., a 20-year-old college sophomore, rarely smokes now because he found he was losing his edge in volleyball and Frisbee games. A 28-year-old dancer who said she smoked heavily in high school takes a drag every couple of years and finds to her disappointment that she becomes paranoid and self-conscious and ends up wondering why she tried it again. Her friend, a graphic artist, said she decided she could not tolerate the loss of hand-eye coordination. A lawyer in her 40's said that while she didn't believe smoking was bad, it began to seem "foolhardy" to risk an arrest that "could wreck your career."

SHUTTERSTOCK

Once available for $20 to $30 an ounce, marijuana has been made a scarce commodity because of relentless police pressure.

Marijuana smoking reached its peak in 1979, when the National Institute on Drug Abuse estimated, based on its survey, that more than 31.5 million Americans had used the drug at least once during that year. By 1990, when the most recent statistics were compiled, the marijuana-smoking crowd had diminished by more than a third, to 20.5 million.

With the nation's population steadily rising, those smoking marijuana in 1990 represented 10.2 percent of all Americans over the age of 12, compared with 17.8 percent in 1979.

More than 66 million people have tried marijuana at least once, compared with 22.7 million who have sampled cocaine, the National Institute on Drug Abuse says. In 1990, the institute estimated that 10.2 million Americans had used marijuana within the last month, compared with 1.6 million who had used cocaine.

These estimates may understate total marijuana use, many drug experts say, but probably accurately reflect a pronounced decline. Even organizations that advocate making marijuana legal and regulating it like alcohol say there has been a significant decrease.

EVEN ROCK FANS LOOK AROUND FIRST

People still smoke marijuana at rock concerts. But they look around before they pull out a joint and they hold off if they see an usher coming. A New York woman studying at the University of Rhode Island said most of her circle of friends smoked marijuana. "But," she added, "it's become much more of a taboo topic, much less socially acceptable. It's gone under the rug."

Back in 1979, almost all the marijuana smoked in the United States was grown in other countries and it all seemed to have romantic names. There were Thai Sticks, Cambodian Red, Colombian Gold, Panama Red and some from Mexico known simply by place names, Oaxaca and Michoacan. The United States Customs Service seized more than 3.5 million pounds of marijuana in 1979. Last year, Federal agents intercepted 222,274 pounds, or one-sixteenth as much.

The great wall of boats, planes and radar thrown up by the Federal Government may not have dented the cocaine trade, but it nearly killed marijuana smuggling. Marijuana is much bulkier and harder to conceal than cocaine and, until recently, it sold for much less.

"We used to call it the Big Green Elephant," said a charter boat captain in Miami. "You could smell it a quarter of a mile away." He, like others with intimate knowledge of the trade, agreed to speak only with the promise of anonymity.

Unable to get through the barriers or unwilling to risk jail for the lower profits from marijuana, some smugglers dropped out; others shifted to cocaine. "For a lot of guys, bringing in a load of marijuana was a form of high adventure," the Miami skipper said. "But it became very dangerous and guys said, 'This is ridiculous.' "

As recently as 1984, the biggest percentage of America's marijuana was from Colombia. Now Mexico is the main foreign supplier and the most sought-after marijuana is grown in California, Oregon and Hawaii.

HOME-GROWN DRUG EMBARRASSES BUSH

The war against domestically grown marijuana accelerated in early 1990, after President Bush was embarrassed at a conference on drugs in Colombia at which Alan Garcia, then President of Peru, suggested that Washington could hardly expect Latin America to stop growing the raw material for cocaine when marijuana farmers flourished in the United States.

Government spray planes wiped out 85 to 90 percent of Hawaii's marijuana, administration officials say. Millions of other marijuana plants were destroyed in national parks and on other public lands that farmers had begun cultivating to avoid the Government's seizing private property used for illegal crops. Scores of greenhouses, each containing hundreds of plants, were raided and Federal agents began tracking marijuana farmers through the records of companies that sell nursery supplies.

"You can't wink at marijuana," said Robert C. Bonner, the chief of the Drug Enforcement Administration. "It is not a benign drug. It affects productivity and general alertness. It has a corruptive influence on law enforcement and public officials. And if we want other countries to control cocaine production, we have to lead by example."

Federal spending to fight marijuana at home nearly doubled in the 1991 fiscal year, to $35 million, and the administration requested $87 million for 1992.

GOLD CLOSED AT $359. GUESS WHAT'S $375?

After the air raids in Hawaii, the retail price of marijuana there leaped from $2,000 a pound to $6,000, which is $375 an ounce, or $16 more than an ounce of gold.

Prices fluctuate around the country, but in the Northeast these days it is not unusual to pay $280 an ounce. Most sales, the dealers say, are of quarter-ounce packets. Street hustlers still offer plastic sandwich bags of what looks like marijuana for $10. But quite often, experienced smokers say, the hustlers are pedaling diluted marijuana or a jumble of nonintoxicating herbs.

As a hedge against being ripped off, many buyers get friends to refer them to reputable dealers. One New York dealer wears a beeper and promises delivery in midtown within half an hour of receiving a telephone order. Another works out of his tasteful apartment on the Upper West Side of Manhattan, offering three grades of marijuana for as much as $800 an ounce.

Cocaine is currently selling in New York for $800 to $1,200 an ounce. The same amount of heroin is fetching more than $5,000.

The Upper West Side dealer's customers are lawyers, doctors, stockbrokers and other well-paid professionals. To them, price is of little consequence. But it does matter to many people.

"If it goes up anymore, I'm going to stop smoking," said an art major at one Northeastern college.

Some marijuana users have turned to growing their own. One professional, for example, has a small garden in a closet of his home on Staten Island. Hundreds if not thousands of other New Yorkers are growing a few marijuana plants on windowsills.

But the best quality comes from plants that require more attention than most people want to give. So a legion of outlaw horticulturists are developing throughout the country. One of them, a young man who lives in Maryland, told of setting up nurseries in the recreation room and basements of three houses not far from Washington, and of tending marijuana bushes on small plots of Government land in the capital.

"D.C. is an excellent growing environment for marijuana," he said. "With all that concrete, it retains about five degrees more heat than the outlying areas and you get approximately one to two weeks more growing time."

Medical Marijuana Use Winning Backing

BY CAREY GOLDBERG | OCT. 30, 1996

THE CLINTON ADMINISTRATION has condemned it as a cynical hoax, the Republican Presidential candidate, Bob Dole, has denounced it as dangerous, and in a letter released today, former Presidents George Bush, Gerald R. Ford and Jimmy Carter call it a threat to the public health of "all Americans."

But in the battle over Proposition 215, the California initiative that would legalize the medical use of marijuana for people with AIDS, cancer and other diseases, polls show voters leaning away from politicians' dire warnings and toward the likes of Anna Boyce, a 67-year-old nurse shown in television advertisements that began appearing this week.

Describing her husband's death from cancer, she tells viewers: "The nausea from his chemotherapy was so awful it broke my heart. So I broke the law and got him marijuana. It worked. He could eat. He had an extra year of life. Proposition 215 will allow patients like J. J. use of marijuana without becoming criminals. Vote yes on 215. God forbid someone you love may need it."

Three recent California polls show a majority siding with Mrs. Boyce and Proposition 215, which would require only a "doctor's recommendation" for marijuana use by patients with AIDS, cancer, glaucoma "or any other illness for which marijuana provides relief."

A Field Poll ending Oct. 9 showed that 56 percent of those surveyed would vote for the measure, a private poll in the same period by the campaign for Proposition 215 found 57 percent supporting it, and a Los Angeles Times poll released last week found 58 percent in favor. The opposition never topped 36 percent in the three polls.

Advocates of tough drug policies are deeply concerned, seeing before them the prospect of a precipitous loosening of control over marijuana use in the nation's most populous state.

"We believe the vote of Californians on Proposition 215 is the most important vote they will cast in the 1996 elections," said Joseph A. Califano Jr., the former Secretary of Health, Education and Welfare who founded the National Center on Addiction and Substance Abuse at Columbia University. In terms of drug policy nationwide, he added, the vote on 215 is "unquestionably the most important vote that will be cast in this election," particularly because California has been a trend-setter on social issues.

The public support for Proposition 215 highlights a shift in public opinion: even the initiative's foes acknowledge that people are siding ever more decisively with the idea that seriously ill patients should have access to anything that will ease their suffering.

A poll commissioned by Mr. Califano's center found that 58 percent of Californians said marijuana should be available to the dying.

But Gen. Barry R. McCaffrey, President Clinton's drug policy director, complains that the initiative goes much further than help for the dying. He issued a strongly worded statement today, calling 215 a "falsely labeled, cynical initiative."

National medical groups have refused to endorse marijuana treatment, he said, adding that the initiative was actually a "stalking horse for legalization" because it did not specify that a doctor's prescription be written. It would also send the message to teen-agers that "marijuana is medicine," he said.

"We should ask ourselves whether we really want Cheech and Chong logic to guide our thinking about medicine," General McCaffrey said.

Mr. Califano's group, which researches drug abuse and seeks to promote public concern over it, on Monday released the results of its own poll, which showed that Californians' support for the initiative had dropped to just 46 percent.

But proponents of the initiative immediately dismissed the survey as a flawed poll that prompted negative results from respondents and deviated too much from others to be credible. They also objected to opponents' warnings that the initiative would open the door to virtually a blanket legalization of marijuana. Patients in Florida and Ohio already have protections similar to those that 215 will provide, they say.

"At a certain point, the other side needs to stop trying to scare people and confuse voters, and we need to start thinking seriously about how this is really going to work in California," said Dave Fratello, a spokesman for the pro-215 campaign, which held its own news conference immediately after Mr. Califano's.

General McCaffrey is not ready to contemplate any such thing. He plans to spend three days in California working with the local police and elected officials to fight the initiative.

A force against the initiative is the mounting alarm nationwide over a recent doubling in marijuana use among teen-agers and voters' concern, as found in the poll sponsored by Mr. Califano's group, that Proposition 215 would lead to increased recreational use of marijuana.

But in its favor there is public sympathy for people like Judith Cushner, a former breast cancer sufferer who described on California television how marijuana had helped her through the pain of chemotherapy. She warned, "Someday, you may need it." In another advertisement, Dr. Richard Cohen, who has defied California law and prescribed marijuana for many cancer patients, says, "Morphine works. Marijuana works. Let us physicians treat you with every medicine that can help."

Backers of the initiative have $750,000 to spend on such commercials in the week before the election, Mr. Fratello said. Opponents have managed to raise only $30,000 overall, leaving them fuming that they have been hobbled by the lack of money for advertisements and that denunciations by politicians like Gov. Pete Wilson and Senator Dianne Feinstein are not enough.

"We've been telling people for months that the only way to stop this is to send some money and let us get on the air," said the manager of the campaign against 215, Stu Mollrich. "And nobody's done it."

5 States Vote Medical Use of Marijuana

BY JAMES BROOKE | NOV. 5, 1998

DEFYING FEDERAL OFFICIALS, and often state legislators, voters approved initiatives on Tuesday to legalize the medical use of marijuana in Alaska, Arizona, Nevada, Oregon and Washington State.

And in Colorado and the District of Columbia, where conservatives nullified medical marijuana initiatives at the last moment, surveys of voters leaving the polls on Tuesday indicated strong support for the measures.

Drug policy analysts said today that the votes, in which every marijuana initiative on a state ballot was approved, demonstrated the sea change in attitudes that started with the approval of ballot measures in Arizona and California in 1996.

"I don't think any of these propositions would have passed five years ago," said Mark A. R. Kleiman, professor of policy studies at the University of California at Los Angeles. "It is no longer possible to buffalo the American people by screaming drugs and having them run away."

But the drives for the initiatives were bolstered by $5 million in advertising over the last year, estimated Ethan Nadelmann, director of the Lindesmith Center, a drug policy institute in New York. The campaign was financed by George Soros, the billionaire investor who financed the Lindesmith Center; Peter B. Lewis, a Cleveland insurance executive, and John Sperling, a Phoenix entrepreneur.

The votes would give confidence to politicians who are afraid to publicly support allowing doctors to recommend marijuana to patients suffering from illnesses like glaucoma, cancer and multiple sclerosis, Mr. Nadelmann predicted.

In Oregon and Arizona, the votes were direct slaps at State Legislatures that had voted curbs on marijuana.

In Oregon, the State Legislature last year restored criminal penalties for marijuana possession. On Tuesday, Oregonians voted, 2 to 1, to make possession merely a violation carrying a fine, as it had been since 1973. They also voted, by a smaller margin, to approve the medical use of marijuana.

In Arizona, the State Legislature had approved bills last year that essentially gutted the marijuana referendum votes of 1996. On Tuesday, Arizona voters easily approved two initiatives that restored the 1996 language.

"In two states, Arizona and Oregon, people overthrew the politicians on drugs," Sam Vagenas, leader of Arizona's medical marijuana movement, said today. "This is the biggest grass-roots movement since term limits."

Opposition to the medical marijuana movement has come from big-city police chiefs, Congress, and the White House's top drug policy official, Gen. Barry R. McCaffrey.

In Senate testimony last summer, the general, who directs the Office of National Drug Control Policy, made a veiled reference to Mr. Soros: "There is a carefully camouflaged, exorbitantly funded, well-heeled elitist group whose ultimate goal is to legalize drug use in the United States."

Today, the general's office emphasized that the state measures "in no way alter the status of marijuana under Federal law."

"We are concerned about the mixed message that children pick up on this," Jim McDonough, director of strategy for the White House drug control office, said today of the advertising campaigns to allow medical uses of medical marijuana. Noting that the number of marijuana users in the nation had dropped by half since 1980, to about 10 million today, he said that surveys indicated a recent increase among students.

In the District of Columbia, Representative Bob Barr, a conservative Republican from Georgia, had inserted into the District's Federal appropriation bill an amendment to bar the District from counting votes in Tuesday's medical marijuana initiative. The American Civil Liberties Union is suing to overturn the ban.

In Colorado, a medical marijuana initiative was also on the ballot, but Vikki Buckley, the Secretary of State and a Republican, said she would not count the votes because the initiative backers did not supply enough valid signatures to place the issue on the ballot. Backers are contesting her ruling in court.

CHAPTER 4

Since 2000: States, and the Public, Embrace Legalization

Starting in the late 1990s, several states began legalizing the use of medical marijuana, a trend that became the norm in the 2000s. In 2013, voters in Colorado and Washington went further, voting to legalize recreational marijuana use. To date, laws regulating cannabis use vary from state to state, and the U.S. federal government still classifies it as a Schedule I drug with no accepted medical use. In 2018, the Canadian legislature voted to legalize recreational cannabis use, making Canada the third nation to do so.

Misguided Marijuana War

EDITORIAL | BY THE NEW YORK TIMES | FEB. 4, 2003

ADMINISTRATION OFFICIALS annoyed at California's support of the medical use of marijuana have found someone on whom to vent their frustration. Last week, at the urging of federal prosecutors, a judge convicted Ed Rosenthal of charges that carry a five-year minimum sentence. Mr. Rosenthal is a medical-marijuana advocate who grows the drug for use by the seriously ill. His harsh punishment shows that the misguided federal war on medical marijuana has now escalated out of control.

Mr. Rosenthal, who raised marijuana in an Oakland warehouse, was acting within state and local law. California's Proposition 215, which voters approved in a 1996 referendum, permits marijuana use by seriously ill people. In addition, Oakland has its own medical marijuana law, and Mr. Rosenthal was acting as an officer of the city. Nevertheless, the judge refused to allow the defense to mention any of this at his trial, since it is not a valid defense against federal drug charges.

Prosecutors were thus able to present Mr. Rosenthal as an ordinary, big-time drug dealer. After a witness said he had met Mr. Rosenthal "in the context of Proposition 215," the judge instructed the jury to disregard the reference, and took over the questioning himself. The foreman said afterward he felt the jury had had no choice but to convict, but hoped Mr. Rosenthal would win on appeal.

The prosecution of Mr. Rosenthal is only the latest attempt by the federal government to frustrate the will of California voters. Washington has also tried to revoke the licenses of doctors who recommend marijuana to their patients. This strategy was struck down as unconstitutional by a federal court last fall.

The Bush administration's war on medical marijuana is not only misguided but mean-spirited. Doctors have long recognized marijuana's value in reducing pain and aiding in the treatment of cancer and AIDS, among other diseases. A recent poll found that 80 percent of Americans support legalized medical marijuana. The reasons the government gives for objecting to it do not outweigh the good it does. And given the lack of success of the war on drugs in recent years, there must be better places to direct law enforcement resources.

If the Bush administration really believes Proposition 215 has no legal authority, it should seek to strike down the law itself. Or it could go after cities like Oakland, which make medical marijuana available as part of municipal policy. Such an approach could be inconvenient for an administration that favors greater autonomy for state and local governments. But it is less vindictive than a strategy that attacks doctors and people like Mr. Rosenthal.

The courts should not allow Mr. Rosenthal's conviction to stand. It would be a serious injustice if he were to serve years in prison, as he well may. Meanwhile, the administration should stop tyrannizing doctors and sick people and focus on more important aspects of the war on drugs.

The World: Up in Smoke; The U.S. Bucks a Trend on Marijuana Laws

BY ERIC SCHLOSSER | JUNE 1, 2003

LAST WEEK, Canada's governing Liberal Party introduced a bill that would decriminalize the possession of up to 15 grams of marijuana. "Cannabis consumption is first and foremost a health matter," Justice Minister Martin Couchon declared. "It should not result in criminal penalties." Under the new plan, a minor pot offense would be punished with a citation and a fine, much like a speeding ticket.

The bill is strongly opposed by the Bush administration, which has threatened to step up drug searches at the border, creating traffic jams and delaying Canadian exports. "It is my job to protect Americans from dangerous threats," John P. Walters, director of the Office of National Drug Control Policy, warned last year, "and right now, Canada is a dangerous staging area for some of the most dangerous marijuana."

The conflict revolves around a question being addressed in other Western nations: should marijuana be legal, illegal — or something in between?

Canada's move to decriminalize is part of a shift in international attitudes toward pot, away from the "reefer madness" legacy. Spain and Italy decriminalized marijuana in the 1990's. Portugal decriminalized it in 2001, Luxembourg and Belgium the next year. In the Netherlands — where pot has been available since 1976 — "pharmaceutical grade" cannabis is provided, free of charge, through the national health service. Britain plans to reduce penalties for possession this summer, a policy supported by the nation's leading medical journal, The Lancet. It concluded, "moderate indulgence in cannabis has little ill effect on health."

Meanwhile, the United States has escalated its war on pot. The number of marijuana arrests now approaches three-quarters of a million annually, largely for simple possession. More people are in prison for marijuana crimes today than ever before. Dozens, if not hundreds, are serving life sentences for nonviolent pot offenses. Attorney General John Ashcroft has called for full enforcement of the pot laws and spearheaded a crackdown on medicinal marijuana providers in California, though their efforts are legal under state law.

The war on marijuana, however, is by no means a partisan affair. It unites Democrats and Republicans in a uniquely American crusade waged on moral grounds.

Though Bill Clinton was the first president to admit having put a joint in his mouth, more people were arrested for marijuana during his administration than under any other American president. Richard M. Nixon may have seemed the nemesis of young pot smokers, but more than three times as many people were arrested for pot while Mr. Clinton was president. "Marijuana is illegal, dangerous, unhealthy and wrong," said Donna E. Shalala, his secretary of health and human services.

The prohibition of marijuana in the United States has historically been driven more by a fear and dislike of people associated with it than by reasoned consideration of its actual harm. The laws have been used to sanction racial minorities and nonconformists. Oddly enough, the first American law about marijuana, passed by the Virginia Assembly in 1619, required every household to grow it. Hemp was considered a valuable commodity.

Popular fears of marijuana arose in the early 20th century, prompted by the use of the drug by Mexican immigrants. Rumors spread about the "killer weed" that incited violent crimes and drove its users insane.

Marijuana was linked not only to poor Mexicans, but also to poor blacks and the new music they played: jazz. Jazz was then regarded much as hip-hop is today in some circles, as a subversive and barbaric threat to the national morality. Not long after marijuana was outlawed in 1937, the Federal Bureau of Narcotics planned to stage a nationwide roundup of black jazz musicians who smoked pot. Harry J. Anslinger, head of the bureau, hated jazz and saw it as a corrupting influence in American life. The plan was thwarted, however, by the inability of its agents to infiltrate the jazz milieu.

First Mexicans, blacks and jazz musicians; then beatniks and hippies; now members of the hip-hop world — marijuana has always been associated with minorities and subcultures that seem to threaten mainstream America. America's marijuana laws usually expressed that fear of outsiders in moralistic terms, while proving ineffective at stopping pot use.

The hippie counterculture of the 1960's rose at a time when America's marijuana laws were at their harshest; in Louisiana, possessing any pot could mean a prison sentence of 99 years. Pot use flourished, as a form of rebellion, and middle-class parents questioned the stiff laws, once their children were jailed for possessing a joint.

The comedians Cheech & Chong became the embodiment of a new stoner culture; far from alarming, it was presented as sweet and ridiculous. In 1972 a commission appointed by President Nixon advocated decriminalizing marijuana, aiming to "desymbolize it." The following year Oregon became the first state to decriminalize pot; 11 other states followed; and President Jimmy Carter supported decriminalization at the federal level. By the end of the 1970's, as marijuana laws were being relaxed in the United States, pot use among teenagers reached its peak and then started to decline.

Moral condemnations of pot smokers and long prison sentences were revived by President Ronald Reagan, as a part of that era's culture wars. Mr. Reagan's first drug czar, Carlton E. Turner, felt that marijuana use was linked to anti-authority behavior and insisted pot could turn young men into homosexuals.

As marijuana use declined among middle-class families, elected officials saw little political gain in opposing the tough drug laws. Many saw strong opposition to marijuana as an easy way to distance themselves from the excesses of the hippie counterculture.

Today, it is largely poor people and minority offenders who are imprisoned for marijuana offenses. Pot smokers can now lose their cars, houses, jobs, student loans and food stamps after getting busted.

The nation's harsh marijuana policy increasingly isolates Washington from many of its allies. In February, the Justice Department staged a nationwide roundup of bong and roach clip manufacturers. Even as the nation feared seemingly imminent attacks by Al Qaeda, an inchoate danger, Attorney General Ashcroft announced the success of "Operation Pipe Dream." Among those arrested was Tommy Chong, who now manufactures a line of bongs.

The symbolism could hardly have been more fitting. Mr. Chong recently plead guilty to a federal conspiracy charge and could face a prison sentence of five years.

ERIC SCHLOSSER is the author of "Reefer Madness: Sex, Drugs and Cheap Labor in the American Black Market."

Canada to Offer Marijuana to Medical Patients

BY CLIFFORD KRAUSS | JULY 10, 2003

THE CANADIAN GOVERNMENT announced an interim plan today that will provide marijuana on a regular basis to several hundred people who are authorized to use the drug for medical reasons.

Coming six weeks after the federal government introduced a bill decriminalizing possession of small amounts of marijuana and only days after it approved a trial "safe injection site" in Vancouver for intravenous drug users, the marijuana plan was one more sign that Ottawa is moving in a very different direction on drug policy from the Bush administration.

Thousands of Canadians already visit so-called "compassion clubs" in Vancouver and a few other cities, which distribute marijuana to those who come with a note from a doctor saying that the drug can help their condition. The police have occasionally entered some of the clinics and seized marijuana, but for the most part they function in the open.

The decision to allow the government to provide marijuana to people with illnesses ranging from cancer to arthritis to epilepsy was forced by a ruling in January by the Ontario Superior Court that federal marijuana access regulations were unconstitutional because they did not provide patients with a legal distribution system.

The government is appealing the ruling, meaning that the announcement may not stand.

"It was never our intention to sell the product," said Health Minister Anne McClellan, a skeptic of medical marijuana use.

The cabinet is divided on whether the government should be growing and distributing marijuana, an activity that is otherwise illegal. Ms. McClellan noted today that there is a lack of clinical evidence that marijuana has medicinal benefits. She added that the government will conduct its own clinical trials, scheduled to begin this fall, to gauge possible benefits.

The government says it intends to distribute the marijuana through doctors. Some officials of doctors associations have raised cautions about doing so before there is more study about the impact of marijuana use on people's health.

While the courts decide on the government's appeal, Ottawa will provide as many as 500 people, who have received letters from doctors saying the drug offered them medical benefits, with dried marijuana and marijuana seeds for their own planting.

The marijuana will cost patients almost $4 a gram, or about half the black market price.

The bags of seeds will cost about $15. The marijuana will come from an underground laboratory situated in an old mine in Flin Flon, Manitoba.

"This is a very small victory but a victory nevertheless," said Alison Myrden, a multiple sclerosis patient who appeared before television cameras today in front of the Parliament building holding a marijuana plant and smoking a marijuana cigarette.

Justices Say U.S. May Prohibit the Use of Medical Marijuana

BY LINDA GREENHOUSE | JUNE 7, 2005

WASHINGTON, JUNE 6 — The Supreme Court on Monday upheld the power of Congress to prohibit and prosecute the possession and use of marijuana for medical purposes, even in the 11 states that permit it.

The 6-to-3 decision, a firm reassertion of federal authority, revealed a deep fissure within the coalition that over the past decade has provided the majority for a series of decisions curbing Congressional power and elevating the role of the states within the federal system. Two members of that coalition, Justices Anthony M. Kennedy and Antonin Scalia, voted this time to uphold federal authority.

The decision overturned a 2003 ruling by a federal appeals court that shielded California's Compassionate Use Act, the medical-marijuana initiative adopted by the state's voters nine years ago, from the reach of federal drug enforcement.

The appeals court had held that Congress lacked constitutional authority to regulate the noncommercial cultivation and use of marijuana that did not cross state lines.

But "the regulation is squarely within Congress's commerce power," Justice John Paul Stevens said for the majority on Monday. He added that the court's precedents interpreting Congress's authority under the Commerce Clause of the Constitution had clearly established "Congress's power to regulate purely local activities that are part of an economic 'class of activities' that have a substantial effect on interstate commerce."

The decision, Gonzales v. Raich, No. 03-1454, was not necessarily the last word on medical marijuana, either from the courts or from other branches of government. Under the terms of the opinion, the United States Court of Appeals for the Ninth Circuit, in San Francisco, will now consider other challenges to the application of federal drug law.

These include an argument made by the two women who brought the case that it is a violation of their constitutional right to due process to deprive them of what they say is the only drug that eases their suffering from a variety of painful conditions.

Because the two patients, Angel McClary Raich and Diane Monson, prevailed in the Ninth Circuit on their Commerce Clause argument, the appeals court did not address the other issues they raised.

Advocates for medical marijuana, meanwhile, emphasized on Monday that the state laws remained in effect, meaning that state officials would not prosecute patients who used medical marijuana, and that the prospect of federal enforcement was fairly remote. Allen Hopper, a lawyer with the Drug Law Reform Project of the American Civil Liberties Union, noted that the federal government handles only about 1 percent of marijuana prosecutions.

Justice Stevens, noting that "perhaps even more important than these legal avenues is the democratic process," suggested that the executive branch might reclassify marijuana for medical purposes or that Congress might take up the matter.

The first option appeared quite unlikely, given the response by John P. Walters, the Bush administration's "drug czar," the director of national drug control policy. "To date, science and research have not determined that smoking a crude plant is safe or effective," his official statement said, adding, "We have a responsibility as a civilized society to ensure that the medicine Americans receive from their doctors is effective, safe and free from the pro-drug politics that are being promoted in America under the guise of medicine."

The House of Representatives is due to vote next week on an appropriations amendment that would prohibit the Justice Department from spending money to enforce federal drug laws against patients using marijuana for medical purposes. While the amendment failed last year, 19 Republicans voted for it. It was not brought to a vote in the Senate.

Mrs. Raich, one of the plaintiffs, speaking along with her husband and lawyers in a telephone news conference, said she would continue to use the marijuana that was prescribed by her doctor and is grown for her by friends. "I don't have a choice but to continue because if I stopped I would die," she said. She suffers from a wasting syndrome, among other ailments, and said that only marijuana gave her the appetite to eat enough to maintain her weight.

The women brought the case after federal agents arrived at Ms. Monson's home in 2002 and, after a three-hour standoff, seized and destroyed her six plants. The two women sued for a declaration that the federal Controlled Substances Act did not apply to their situation.

The opinion by Justice Stevens was joined by his allies in many recent battles over federalism, Justices David H. Souter, Ruth Bader Ginsburg and Stephen G. Breyer, and by Justice Kennedy, who did not provide an explanation for his vote.

Justice Scalia, by contrast, explained himself at length. He did not sign the majority opinion, instead offering a separate concurring opinion that was no less definite in its support for federal authority.

"Where necessary to make a regulation of interstate commerce effective, Congress may regulate even those intrastate activities that do not themselves substantially affect interstate commerce," Justice Scalia said. He cited opinions from the early 1940's, after the Supreme Court rallied to support the New Deal and gave Congress a degree of power over national affairs that was not seriously challenged until the Rehnquist Court began invalidating federal laws in the mid-1990's.

Chief Justice Rehnquist was one of the dissenters on Monday. He and Justice Clarence Thomas joined a dissenting opinion by Justice Sandra Day O'Connor; Justice Thomas also wrote a separate dissenting opinion.

As a prime mover of the court's federalism revolution, Justice O'Connor did not hide her dismay. The court's opinion provided a roadmap to "removing meaningful limits on the Commerce Clause" and "threatens to sweep all of productive human activity into federal regulatory reach," she said.

Justice O'Connor said that while she did not support the medical marijuana initiative as public policy, it represented the kind of innovation and "experiment" that came within the latitude the Constitution allows the states.

"The states' core police powers have always included authority to define criminal law and to protect the health, safety and welfare of their citizens," she said, adding that "whatever the wisdom of California's experiment with medical marijuana, the federalism principles that have driven our Commerce Clause cases require that room for experiment be protected in this case."

Justice Thomas said that "if Congress can regulate this under the Commerce Clause, then it can regulate virtually anything, and the federal government is no longer one of limited and enumerated powers."

The sharpest dispute was over the meaning of two of the core decisions of the Rehnquist Court's approach to federalism. Both struck down federal laws, the Gun-Free School Zones Act and the Violence Against Women Act, on the ground that they exceeded Congressional authority, and both were decided by five-member majorities that included Justices Kennedy and Scalia.

While Justice O'Connor declared that the marijuana decision was "irreconcilable" with the earlier ones, Justice Scalia disagreed. Neither of the earlier decisions "involved the power of Congress to exert control over intrastate activities in connection with a more comprehensive scheme of regulation" comparable to federal drug laws, he said.

Besides California, states allowing use of marijuana for medical purposes are Alaska, Arizona, Colorado, Hawaii, Maine, Montana, Nevada, Oregon, Washington and Vermont.

U.S. Won't Prosecute in States That Allow Medical Marijuana

BY DAVID STOUT AND SOLOMON MOORE | OCT. 19, 2009

WASHINGTON — People who use marijuana for medical purposes and those who distribute it to them should not face federal prosecution, provided they act according to state law, the Justice Department said Monday in a directive with far-reaching political and legal implications.

In a memorandum to federal prosecutors in the 14 states that make some allowance for the use of marijuana for medical purposes, the department said that it was committed to the "efficient and rational use" of its resources and that prosecuting patients and distributors who are in "clear and unambiguous compliance" with state laws did not meet that standard.

The new stance was hardly an enthusiastic embrace of medical marijuana, or the laws that allow it in some states, but signaled clearly that the administration thought there were more important priorities for prosecutors.

"It will not be a priority to use federal resources to prosecute patients with serious illnesses or their caregivers who are complying with state laws on medical marijuana," Attorney General Eric H. Holder Jr. said in a statement accompanying the memo, "but we will not tolerate drug traffickers who hide behind claims of compliance with state law to mask activities that are clearly illegal."

Emphasizing that it would continue to pursue those who use the concept of medical marijuana as a ruse, the department said, "Marijuana distribution in the United States remains the single largest source of revenue for the Mexican cartels," and pursuing the makers and sellers of illegal drugs, including marijuana, will remain a "core priority."

The politics swirling around marijuana cross ideological lines. For instance, in effectively deferring to the states on some issues involving marijuana, the Obama administration is taking what could be seen as a states' rights stance, more commonly associated with conservatives. That was a theme that echoed on many conservative and libertarian Internet sites in the wake of Monday's announcement.

But one prominent conservative, Representative Lamar Smith of Texas, criticized the Justice Department's position, saying it would weaken federal enforcement of drug laws.

"By directing federal law enforcement officers to ignore federal drug laws, the administration is tacitly condoning the use of marijuana in the United States," said Mr. Smith, the senior Republican on the House Judiciary Committee. "If we want to win the war on drugs, federal prosecutors have a responsibility to investigate and prosecute all medical marijuana dispensaries and not just those that are merely fronts for illegal marijuana distribution."

Polls have shown for years that there is widespread public support for making marijuana available to relieve the suffering of people who are very ill. But repeated efforts in Congress to block federal prosecution of medical marijuana have fallen short, and the new policy was a sharp departure from that of the Bush administration, in which the Drug Enforcement Administration raided medical marijuana distributors even if the distributors appeared to be complying with state laws.

The new policy, which reflects positions that Mr. Obama took as a presidential candidate and that Mr. Holder laid out in March, came in a memo from David W. Ogden, the deputy attorney general, to the United States attorneys in the affected states, most notably California.

The White House sought to turn aside any impression that Mr. Obama would like other states to follow the example of the 14 that make some allowance for medical marijuana.

"I'm not going to get into what states should do," said the president's chief spokesman, Robert Gibbs.

Mr. Gibbs said the memo to federal prosecutors "simply adds guidelines to a decision that Attorney General Holder talked about in

CHRISTOPHER CAPOZZIELLO FOR THE NEW YORK TIMES

Rob Mooney, 49, of East Providence, R.I., uses medical marijuana to ease severe back pain.

mid-March and has been administration policy since the beginning of this administration in January."

The guidelines give specific examples of conduct that would cause prosecutors to look at a case involving marijuana even if a user or distributor said it was for medical use. The examples include unlawful possession or use of a firearm, sales to minors and evidence of money laundering activity.

Graham Boyd, director of the Drug Law Reform Project at the American Civil Liberties Union, called the Justice Department's move "an enormous step in the right direction and, no doubt, a great relief to the thousands of Americans who benefit from the medical use of marijuana."

Mr. Boyd predicted that states and cities "will have a strong incentive to create regulated, safe and sensible means of getting marijuana to patients who need it."

The new policy follows a series of changes, including the appointment of Richard Gil Kerlikowske, a former police chief of Seattle, to be Mr. Obama's top drug policy adviser.

Medical marijuana thrived in Seattle on Mr. Kerlikowske's watch, and advocates of more liberal marijuana laws hoped that his appointment to the office, which he assumed in May, signaled the administration's willingness to decriminalize medical marijuana.

Some federal law enforcement officials are opposed to the administration's position.

Privately, some federal law enforcement officials complained that medical marijuana and marijuana being smuggled in from Mexico are one and the same, and that the Obama administration has backed away from necessary enforcement of drug laws. Agents from the D.E.A. often work alongside local police officers.

As Mr. Ogden's memo was being made public, the Web site of the Drug Enforcement Administration outlined its position on medical marijuana: "Smoked marijuana has not withstood the rigors of science — it is not medicine and it is not safe. D.E.A. targets criminals engaged in cultivation and trafficking, not the sick and dying."

Advocates of medical marijuana say it can reduce chronic pain, nausea and additional symptoms associated with cancer and other serious illnesses. In 1996, California became the first state to make it legal to sell marijuana to people with doctors' prescriptions. The other states that allow some use of marijuana for medical purposes are Alaska, Colorado, Hawaii, Maine, Maryland, Michigan, Montana, Nevada, New Mexico, Oregon, Rhode island, Vermont and Washington.

SOLOMON MOORE contributed reporting from Los Angeles.

Legalizing of Marijuana Raises Health Concerns

BY RONI CARYN RABIN | JAN. 7, 2013

IN THE '60S, marijuana was a hallmark of the counterculture, along with free love, bell bottoms, long hair and bandannas. But marijuana has had the most staying power.

This month, in a remarkable first, the recreational use of marijuana became legal (depending on your definition) in Colorado and Washington. Over a dozen other states have decriminalized possession of small amounts, and Massachusetts recently became the 18th state to allow its use for medicinal purposes.

Though federal law still bans both the sale and possession of marijuana, President Obama has said the federal government has "bigger fish to fry" and won't aggressively prosecute tokers in states where its use is legal.

The rise of marijuana as an adult pastime is a victory for those who've always felt that its hazards were overblown. Proponents of legalization argue that marijuana is much safer to use than alcohol, pointing out that it is virtually impossible to overdose on marijuana.

While marijuana can be addictive, scientists generally agree that fewer than 10 percent of marijuana smokers become dependent on the drug, compared with 15 percent for alcohol, 23 percent for heroin and 32 percent for tobacco. Marijuana does contain carcinogens, including tar and other toxins similar to those found in tobacco, but people generally do not smoke marijuana in the same amounts as cigarettes.

Still, legalization takes health consumers into murky territory. Even though marijuana is the most commonly used illegal drug in the United States, questions about its health effects remain.

For starters, this is not your parents' pot. Today's marijuana is much more potent: The mean concentration of THC, the psychoactive ingredient, in confiscated cannabis more than doubled between 1993 and 2008.

Increased potency may be having unforeseen consequences. The human brain's cannabinoid receptors are typically activated by naturally occurring chemicals in the body called endocannabinoids, which are similar to THC. There is a high density of cannabinoid receptors in parts of the brain that affect pleasure, memory and concentration. Some research suggests that these areas continue to be affected by marijuana use even after the "high" dissipates.

"It's much more potent marijuana, which may explain why we've seen a pretty dramatic increase in admission to emergency rooms and treatment programs for marijuana," said Dr. Nora D. Volkow, director of the National Institute on Drug Abuse. "When we hear, 'Well, I smoked and nothing happened to me,' we need to think about the context of when these people started to take it, how frequently they used and how active the marijuana was."

Those in favor of legalizing marijuana say the increase in potency has been exaggerated, and that when users have more powerful pot, they adjust their consumption and actually smoke less.

Teenagers may be more vulnerable to addiction, however, and those who start smoking pot at a younger age are at higher risk. Approximately one in six will become addicted, Dr. Volkow said. Young adults who start smoking marijuana at earlier ages also tend to smoke much more, and more often, than those who start in their later teens, researchers say.

In users who develop a dependence or addiction, quitting can cause intense withdrawal symptoms, like anxiety, trouble sleeping, lack of appetite, mood swings, irritability and depression, experts say.

Both Colorado and Washington restricted marijuana use to adults age 21 and over when they legalized recreational use in November. But experts worry that the perception of marijuana is changing because its stigma as an outlawed drug has eroded.

"When people can go to a 'clinic' or 'cafe' and buy pot, that creates the perception that it's safe," said Dr. A. Eden Evins, director of the Center for Addiction Medicine at Massachusetts General Hospital in

Boston. “Before we unleash the powers of the marketplace to woo people to use this addictive substance, we need to better understand who is at risk.”

“Once moneyed interests are involved, this trend will be difficult to reverse,” she added.

The most disturbing new studies about early teenage use of marijuana showed that young adults who started smoking pot regularly before they were 16 performed significantly worse on cognitive tests of brain function than those who had started smoking later in adolescence. They performed particularly poorly on tests assessing executive function, which is responsible for planning and abstract thinking, as well as understanding rules and inhibiting inappropriate responses.

Imaging scans also found detectable differences in how their brains worked, said Staci Gruber, the lead author of these studies and director of the cognitive and clinical neuroimaging core at the imaging center at McLean Hospital in Boston. Imaging scans found alterations in the frontal cortex white matter tracts of the brain in the early-starters, she said, that are associated with impulsiveness.

“The frontal cortex is the last part of the brain to come online, and the most important,” Dr. Gruber said. “Early exposure perhaps changes the trajectory of brain development, such that ability to perform complex executive function tasks is compromised.”

A recent study showing a drop in IQ scores among teenagers who are regular pot smokers is especially troubling, Dr. Evins said. A more recent study found that people who started smoking marijuana as teenagers and used it heavily for decades lost IQ points over time, while those who started smoking as adults did not, though some critics have said these differences may not be meaningful. Older survey studies had indicated that regular pot smokers were less likely to graduate from high school or pursue higher education, but it was never clear which came first, difficulty in school or the drug use.

“If parents who are spending thousands of dollars on SAT prep courses knew about the cognitive effects marijuana has on their kids’ brains, they would be up in arms," Dr. Evins said. Other health concerns about marijuana are less well documented but may turn out to be significant. States that legalized marijuana prohibit driving under its influence, and studies have found marijuana smoking increases weaving between lanes and slows reaction times. And although marijuana is not as damaging to the lungs as tobacco, in part because people do not smoke a pack of joints a day, a regular habit can eventually take a toll on the lungs.

At the very least, the new studies suggest parents who recall their own pot parties may want to suggest greater moderation to their children. And teenagers who insist on trying marijuana are better off waiting until they're older.

"It's the same message as with alcohol," Dr. Gruber said. "Just hold on, it's worth it to wait."

Up Early and in Line for a Marijuana Milestone in Colorado

BY JACK HEALY | JAN. 1, 2014

DENVER — They lined up before dawn and in the snow on Wednesday, baby boomers from Nebraska, retirees from Denver and a young man who had driven all day from Ohio. Some were longtime marijuana users. Some had been arrested for marijuana possession.

They were among the hundreds of tourists and residents across Colorado who eagerly took part in the country's first-ever sales of state-regulated recreational marijuana. They walked into 40 shops, from downtown Denver to snowy ski resorts, flashed their identifications and, in a single transaction, took part in what supporters hailed as a historic departure from drug laws focused on punishment and prohibition.

"It makes you giddy to say it: I went into a store and bought pot," Linda Walmsley said as she walked out of the Denver Kush Club, where a line of shivering customers stretched down the block.

While about 20 states allow medical marijuana, voters in Colorado and Washington State decided last year to go one step further, becoming the first in the nation to legalize small amounts of the plant for recreational use and regulate it like alcohol. Colorado began promptly on New Year's Day.

To supporters, it was a watershed moment in the country's tangled relationship with the drug. They said it was akin to the end of Prohibition, albeit with joints being passed instead of Champagne being uncorked.

To skeptics, it represented a grand folly that they predicted would tarnish the image of a state whose official song is John Denver's "Rocky Mountain High" and lead to higher teenage drug use and more impaired driving. The governor and the Denver mayor both opposed legalization and stayed away from the celebrations and inaugural sales on Wednesday.

Regulators said Colorado's first sales — on a day called Green Wednesday by enthusiasts — went smoothly. Security guards were stationed outside dispensaries, and police officers and state officials watched closely.

Skeptical federal authorities are also paying attention. Although marijuana remains illegal under federal law, the Justice Department has given tentative approval for Colorado and Washington to move ahead with regulating marijuana. But it warned that federal officials could intervene if the state regulations failed to keep the drug away from children, drug cartels or federal property, and out of other states.

On Wednesday, Colorado had eight investigators out checking retailers' licenses, inspecting packaging and labeling, and ensuring that stores reviewed customers' identification to see if they were 21 or older, said Ron Kammerzell, the director of enforcement for Colorado's Department of Revenue.

"So far, so good," he said.

Ever since voters in Colorado and Washington approved recreational marijuana last year, the states have been racing to devise rules on how to grow it, sell it, tax it and track it.

In both Colorado and Washington, recreational marijuana has been legal for more than a year. Adults can smoke it in their living rooms and eat marijuana-laced cookies without fear of arrest. In Colorado, they are even allowed to grow up to six plants at home. But until Wednesday, marijuana dispensaries could sell only to customers with a doctor's recommendation and a state-issued medical marijuana card.

Many people who lined up on Wednesday said they did not have medical cards, and had relied on drug dealers or friends with medical marijuana to satisfy their cravings. They were paying high prices for new recreational marijuana — $50 to $60 for an eighth of an ounce, nearly double the price of medical marijuana — but said it was worthwhile to avoid the risk.

"People don't like breaking the law," said Andy Williams, who runs the Medicine Man dispensary in an industrial park in Denver. "The burden has been taken off them."

Now, any Colorado resident who is at least 21 can buy up to an ounce of marijuana at one of the dispensaries that began selling to retail customers on Wednesday. Out-of-state visitors can buy a quarter-ounce, but they have to consume it here. Carrying marijuana across state lines remains illegal, and the plant is not allowed at Denver International Airport.

On Wednesday, some tourists puzzled over where they would consume their purchases. It is illegal to smoke marijuana in public, in public parks or in campgrounds, and it is against the rules at many hotels. One group from Nebraska said it would find a parking lot and roll up the car windows. Others said they would return to their hotels and crack the windows. Some bought marijuana-laced baked goods to avoid the problem altogether.

Kirstin Knouse, 24, flew here from Chicago with her husband, Tristan, to take her first marijuana vacation, and she said the couple would smoke their marijuana at the home of a cousin. She said that she suffered from seizures and fibromyalgia, and her husband from post-traumatic stress, but that they had not been able to get medical marijuana at home. When Colorado opened sales to out-of-state residents, she said they leapt at the chance.

"This is our dream," Ms. Knouse said. "We're thinking about moving here because of it."

Washington's marijuana system is at least several months behind Colorado's, meaning that fully stocked retail shelves probably will not be a reality for consumers until perhaps June.

While Colorado has incorporated the existing medical marijuana system, Washington is starting from scratch, with all production and sale of legal recreational marijuana linked to a new system of licenses, which will not be issued until late February or early March.

"After that, it is up to the industry to get it up and running," said Mikhail Carpenter, a spokesman for the Washington State Liquor Control Board, which regulates the system and is reviewing almost 5,000 license applications to grow, process or sell marijuana.

Growers can start a crop only after they get a license, Mr. Carpenter said, and retailers can sell only marijuana produced in the state by licensed growers.

What happens next in both states will be watched closely by Arizona, Alaska, California, Oregon and other states flirting with the idea of liberalizing their marijuana laws. Questions still abound. Will drug traffickers take marijuana across state lines, to sell elsewhere? Will recreational marijuana flow from the hands of legal adult consumers to teenagers? Will taxes from marijuana sales match optimistic predictions of a windfall for state budgets? What will happen to the black market for marijuana?

But on Wednesday, enthusiasts like Darren Austin, 44, and his son, Tyler, 21, just embraced the moment. They arrived a few months ago from Georgia and North Carolina, respectively, and decided to stay. The father said marijuana eased his anxiety and helped him quit drinking, and the son said he simply liked smoking it with friends. On Wednesday, they slept in their truck outside a dispensary, to ensure their place in line.

"We wanted to be here," Darren Austin said. "It's historic."

KIRK JOHNSON contributed reporting from Seattle.

Still-Divided Washington Prepares for Start of Recreational Marijuana Sales

BY KIRK JOHNSON | JULY 6, 2014

VANCOUVER, WASH. — John Larson, a recently retired high school science and math teacher, hopes to be in the first wave of legal recreational marijuana salespeople opening shop here in Washington State this week.

Mr. Larson, 67, who was talked into the venture by his children, said he had never tried marijuana, and, in fact, voted against legalizing it in 2012. But as a business idea — well, that's different.

"If people were dumb enough to vote it in, I'm all for it," he said over a cup of coffee near his shop here in southern Washington, just across the Columbia River from Portland, Ore. "There's a demand, and I have a product."

After nearly two years of anticipation, excitement and dread by still-divided Washington residents, the first licenses for legal sale of recreational marijuana will be issued Monday, state officials said. Sales are to start about 24 hours later.

But the rollout is not unfolding as anyone quite expected it to, from the seemingly unlikely businesspeople like Mr. Larson who are leading the charge to the downright odd pattern of where the first shops will open.

Seattle, for example, with a population of 652,000 the state's largest city and perhaps most marijuana-friendly, will have only a single store initially, and a tiny one at that: 620 square feet, called Cannabis City. But Vancouver, about one-fourth Seattle's size, in a largely conservative county that has tried to slow or stop marijuana businesses with strict land-use rules, could have three shops. Tacoma, also in a county that has tried to block marijuana businesses, may have four.

The pattern came down to chance and circumstance, said Mikhail Carpenter, a spokesman for the Washington State Liquor Control Board, which wrote the regulations and administers the system. With

CARL KIILSGAARD FOR THE NEW YORK TIMES

Main Street Marijuana in downtown Vancouver, Wash., is opening in a former jewelry store. "Light, open and friendly" is the goal, a manager said.

multiple inspections and requirements to meet, "a lot of people weren't ready," Mr. Carpenter said.

Only about 20 licenses out of 334 authorized by the regulations will be granted in this first wave, Mr. Carpenter said, with many would-be operators slowed by financing troubles, inspection questions or other issues. Mr. Larson, for example, applied for three licenses in three cities, and two were denied, in each case because state inspectors said the boundary line was too close to a licensed day care center.

He disagreed, but quickly gave up: "You can't argue with the state."

And even the shops that open will not have that much to sell, because marijuana growers got their licenses only in March, not enough time to produce a big crop. Mr. Larson expects to have perhaps two pounds, which he expects could be gone in hours, and no edible products at all, since no state-licensed marijuana food producers are up and running.

Some retailers said they planned to ration supplies in the early days, allowing customers to buy only a small fraction of the ounce that the law allows for adults over 21.

Low supply in turn means high prices, at least at first, with an ounce — should anyone even be able to buy one — expected to cost at least $400. That is much more than a buyer would typically pay on the black market here in Washington, according to The Price of Weed, a website that surveys marijuana prices by state.

But in some ways, people like Mr. Larson put the most distinctive stamp on Washington's halting first steps. Voters in Colorado approved marijuana legalization at the same time that Washington did in 2012, but then went down a much different regulatory path that pushed things faster, with stores open since January.

Colorado also created the first recreational marijuana shops from the medical marijuana dispensaries that were already in business, which meant that many of the first wave of operators were already in the marijuana trade.

Washington, by contrast, started from scratch, throwing open the application process and giving medical marijuana dispensary operators no edge in the competition for licenses.

In the little town of Prosser, population 5,800, in south central Washington, for example, two chiropractors formed a partnership and hope to open this week. In Seattle, a former restaurant and bar owner is expected to get the first license.

Ramsey Hamide, a manager of Main Street Marijuana, a shop here in downtown Vancouver that plans to open Wednesday, came into the business from the concert ticket industry. He and the other manager, Chris Stipe, are setting up shop in a former jewelry store after visiting more than 20 shops in Colorado to look for ideas.

"We saw what to do — and also what not to do," Mr. Hamide said. Anything that felt confining in particular — security doors and waiting areas for access into the product displays, a common setup for medical dispensaries — was rejected, he said.

CARL KIILSGAARD FOR THE NEW YORK TIMES

John Larson, a recently retired high-school teacher, hopes to be in the first wave of legal recreational marijuana salespeople opening shop in Washington State this week.

"Keep it light, open and friendly," he said of their design plan.

And while many of the new business operators are brimming with optimism about the new market, others say the road ahead might be harder than people want to believe. Protesters in Prosser, for example, have been regularly picketing the chiropractic office of Tim Thompson, a co-owner of the town's marijuana shop, Altitude, carrying signs with slogans like "God Judges Sin."

Initiative 502, which legalized recreational marijuana, passed with 55 percent of the vote statewide, but lost in much of central and eastern Washington.

"They camp out in front of my office every day," Mr. Thompson said in a telephone interview.

Mr. Larson, who said his son had also gone into the business, as a grower, is also braced for a legal fight even as sales begin. His shop has a Vancouver address, and the city has been accepting marijuana businesses, he said, but the shop is on the boundary with an unincorporated area of Clark County, where different rules apply. So Mr. Larson said he planned to be ready to go to court on the opening day of business to fend off any efforts to close him down.

Whatever happens, though, he said, will certainly make for an interesting adventure, and after 35 years of teaching he said he was ready.

"My retirement date is when they close the lid on my coffin," he said.

Recreational Pot Is Officially Legal in California

BY THOMAS FULLER | JAN. 1, 2018

OAKLAND, CALIF. — Retail cannabis shops in California opened their doors on Monday for the first time, inaugurating what proponents say will become the world's largest market for legalized recreational marijuana.

A transaction that remains illegal in many parts of the country seemed almost banal on Monday for the customers at a dispensary in Oakland who picked out their marijuana, showed their driver's licenses and walked into the brisk morning air with their drugs in a paper bag.

"This is a whole new world opening up," said Diana Gladden, 48, who bought marijuana for herself and her aging parents. "My mother, a very strict Southern Baptist, now thinks it's O.K. because it's legal."

One customer left with more than $1,000 worth of cannabis in a large grocery bag.

Medical marijuana has been legal in California for more than two decades but the arrival of full legalization in the state is a milestone for the nation's fast-growing cannabis industry. Pot is now sold legally down the entire length of the West Coast, plus Alaska.

A slow and halting rollout of California's new cannabis regulations limited the number of shops offering the drug on Monday to just a handful of cities across the state, including Berkeley, Oakland, San Jose and San Diego. But more municipalities, including San Francisco and Los Angeles, are expected to issue licenses soon.

Alex Traverso, a spokesman for California's Bureau of Cannabis Control, said around 100 dispensaries in the state were licensed to sell recreational cannabis on Monday.

Outside the dispensary in Oakland nearly 200 people waited in line before dawn for the 6 a.m. start of sales.

JIM WILSON/THE NEW YORK TIMES

People lined up before dawn outside a cannabis dispensary in Oakland, Calif., on Monday.

"Happy New Year!" Steve DeAngelo, the executive director of the dispensary, shouted through a bullhorn. "We've been looking forward to this day for a long time."

But in a state where marijuana has been widely available for so long, the enthusiasm was relatively muted. Outside a dispensary in neighboring Berkeley only a handful of customers waited in line before sales began.

California is the sixth state to introduce the sale of recreational marijuana, after Colorado, Washington, Oregon, Alaska and Nevada. Massachusetts and potentially Maine are expected to begin sales this year.

Legalization here may further raise tensions between the state and federal drug enforcement officials led by Attorney General Jeff Sessions, a vocal opponent of legalization. The federal Drug Enforcement Administration considers marijuana a Schedule 1 drug, the same category as heroin.

JIM WILSON/THE NEW YORK TIMES

A customer, right, at the dispensary purchased more than $1,000 worth of products.

National opinion polls have shown a gradual and steady approval of legalization. Californians voted for recreational use of the drug by a 57 to 43 percent margin in a November 2016 ballot initiative. The law prohibits smoking in public, although such bans are already commonplace in California cities.

Unlike the other states that have legalized, California has a vast industry producing the drug, much of which is illegally sold across state lines. By one estimate, California produces seven times more marijuana than it consumes.

Legalization here will test whether that vast black market of growers, many of whom have been reluctant to join the legal market, will come out of the shadows.

It is unclear how much legalization will increase consumption of the drug in California. Since 1996 marijuana has been available from medical dispensaries for adults with an easily obtainable recommendation card. And even those without medical cards have had little fear of prosecution. It has been many years since police officers in California made arrests for possession of small amounts of marijuana, according to Jennifer Tejada, the chairwoman of the law and legislative committee of the California Police Chief Association.

Jonathan Duenas, a college student and one of the cannabis customers in Oakland on Monday, said he had come for the novelty but probably would not return.

"I have a friend who grows it," he said. "I can get it much cheaper."

Even as more cities in California prepare to issue cannabis licenses, a number of questions remain about the effects and implementation of the new laws.

The head of the Bureau of Cannabis Control has raised concerns that there may not be enough licensed cannabis distributors in the early days of retail sales. A similarly bumpy rollout took place in Nevada in July when the governor, Brian Sandoval, took emergency measures to combat a shortage of legal marijuana soon after legal sales began.

Opponents of legalization warn that California could see an increase in traffic deaths, as appears to have happened in Colorado since stores in that state began selling recreational cannabis four years ago.

Traffic deaths in Colorado involving drivers who tested positive for marijuana more than doubled from 2013 to 2016, according to a study published by a federal government agency in October. The report also noted a 35 percent increase in emergency room visits related to marijuana.

California has not yet adopted a standard measure for marijuana impairment, an issue highlighted on Christmas Eve when a California highway patrolman was killed after a man whom the police said was driving under the influence of both alcohol and marijuana rammed into the back of the officer's vehicle.

A Perplexing Marijuana Side Effect Relieved by Hot Showers

BY RONI CARYN RABIN | APRIL 5, 2018

BY THE TIME Thomas Hodorowski made the connection between his marijuana habit and the bouts of pain and vomiting that left him incapacitated every few weeks, he had been to the emergency room dozens of times, tried anti-nausea drugs, anti-anxiety medications and antidepressants, endured an upper endoscopy procedure and two colonoscopies, seen a psychiatrist and had his appendix and gallbladder removed.

The only way to get relief for the nausea and pain was to take a hot shower.

He often stayed in the shower for hours at a time and could be in and out of the shower for days.

When the hot water ran out, "the pain was unbearable, like somebody was wringing my stomach out like a washcloth," said the 28-year-old, who works as a production and shipping assistant and lives outside Chicago.

It was nearly 10 years until a doctor finally convinced him the diagnosis was cannabinoid hyperemesis syndrome, a condition that causes cyclic vomiting in heavy marijuana users and can be cured by quitting marijuana.

Until recently the syndrome was thought to be uncommon or even rare. But as marijuana use has increased, emergency room physicians say they have been seeing a steady flow of patients with the telltale symptoms, especially in states where marijuana has been decriminalized and patients are more likely to divulge their drug use to physicians.

"After marijuana was legalized in Colorado, we had a doubling in the number of cases of cyclic vomiting syndrome we saw," many of which were probably related to marijuana use, said Dr. Cecilia

JOSHUA LOTT FOR THE NEW YORK TIMES

Thomas Hodorowski quit smoking marijuana after learning his years-long bouts of nausea and vomiting were caused by his habit.

J. Sorensen, an emergency room doctor at University of Colorado Hospital at the Anschutz medical campus in Aurora who has studied the syndrome.

"C.H.S. went from being something we didn't know about and never talked about to a very common problem over the last five years," said Dr. Eric Lavonas, director of emergency medicine at Denver Health and a spokesman for the American College of Emergency Physicians.

Now a new study, based on interviews with 2,127 adult emergency room patients under 50 at Bellevue, a large public hospital in New York City, found that of the 155 patients who said they smoked marijuana at least 20 days a month, 51 heavy users said they had during the past six months experienced nausea and vomiting that were specifically relieved by hot showers.

Extrapolating from those findings, the authors estimated that up to 2.7 million of the 8.3 million Americans known to smoke marijuana on a daily or near-daily basis may suffer from at least occasional bouts of C.H.S.

"The big news is that it's not a couple of thousand people who are affected — it's a couple million people," said Dr. Joseph Habboushe, an assistant professor of emergency medicine at N.Y.U. Langone/ Bellevue Medical Center and lead author of the new paper, published in Basic & Clinical Pharmacology & Toxicology.

Others questioned the one-in-three figure, however. Paul Armentano, the deputy director for the National Organization for the Reform of Marijuana Laws (NORML), said that even with more widespread use of marijuana, "this phenomenon is comparatively rare and seldom is reported" and strikes only "a small percentage of people."

And several physicians who routinely prescribe medicinal marijuana for conditions ranging from chronic pain to epilepsy said they have not seen the cyclic vomiting syndrome in their patients, but noted that they typically prescribe compounds that are not designed to produce a high and contain very low amounts of the psychoactive ingredient THC.

Dr. Habboushe said doctors in other parts of the country may be unfamiliar with C.H.S. or mistake it for a psychiatric or anxiety related syndrome. And even if they are aware of it, many regard it as a "rare, kind of funny disease," replete with anecdotes of patients who spend hours in the shower.

But the condition can be quite serious. One 33-year-old military veteran who asked not to be identified by name described bouts lasting up to 12 hours in which he felt "like a puffer fish with sharp spikes was inflating and driving spikes into my spine from both sides. I've broken bones, and this blew it out of the water."

"I know patients who have lost their jobs, gone bankrupt from repeatedly seeking medical care, and have been misdiagnosed for years," Dr. Habboushe said.

"Marijuana is probably safer than a lot of other things out there, but the discussion about it has been so politicized and the focus has been on the potential benefits, without looking rigorously at what the potential downside might be," he said. "No medication is free from side effects."

Patients often arrive at the hospital severely dehydrated from the combination of hot showers and the inability to keep food or liquids down, and that can lead to acute kidney injury, said Dr. Habboushe.

But since many patients develop the syndrome only after many years of smoking pot, they don't make the connection with their pot habit and have a hard time accepting the diagnosis.

The confusion is understandable, Dr. Sorensen said. "Marijuana is viewed as medicinal, and it's given to people with cancer and AIDS. People know it's used to help with nausea and stimulate the appetite, so it's difficult to get patients to accept that it may be causing their nausea and vomiting."

It's unclear why marijuana can produce such discordant effects in some users. But Dr. Sorensen often tells patients that it's similar to developing an allergy to a favorite food.

Getting the right diagnosis often takes a long time. The average patient makes seven trips to the emergency room, sees five doctors and is hospitalized four times before a definitive diagnosis is made, running up approximately $100,000 in medical bills, Dr. Sorensen's study found.

"They get really expensive workups, lots of CT scans and sometimes exploratory surgery" to rule out dangerous conditions like appendicitis or a bowel obstruction, Dr. Sorensen said. "At the end of the day they're told, 'You're smoking too much pot.' "

The symptoms of C.H.S. often do not respond to drug treatment, though some physicians have had success with the antipsychotic haloperidol (sold under the brand name Haldol) and with capsaicin cream.

The good news is that C.H.S. has a pretty simple cure: abstinence. Patients stop having pain and vomiting episodes when they quit smoking, experts say. And if they start smoking again, they are likely to have a recurrence.

Mr. Hodorowski said he quit smoking once he accepted that marijuana was the cause of his problems, but acknowledges he was in denial for a long time. Now, he says, he's telling his story so other people can learn from his experience.

"I hope they'll be honest with themselves so they don't have to go through what I've been through," he said. "I'm very lucky to have survived this."

F.D.A. Panel Recommends Approval of Cannabis-Based Drug for Epilepsy

BY SHEILA KAPLAN | APRIL 19, 2018

WASHINGTON — A Food and Drug Administration advisory panel on Thursday unanimously recommended approval of an epilepsy medication made with an ingredient found in marijuana. If the agency follows the recommendation, as is expected, the drug would be the first cannabis-derived prescription medicine available in the United States.

The drug, called Epidiolex, is made by GW Pharmaceuticals, a British company. Its active ingredient, cannabidiol, also called CBD, is one of the chemical compounds found in the cannabis plant, but it does not contain the properties that make people high.

That makes it different from the "medical marijuana" allowed by a growing number of states. In those cases, certain patients are legally authorized to smoke or ingest marijuana to treat severe pain, nausea and other ailments.

There are already several drugs on the market that are derived from synthetic versions of THC and other chemicals of the cannabis plant, generally used to ease nausea in cancer patients, and to help AIDS patients avoid weight loss.

Advocates for development of marijuana-based treatments, and those pushing for better treatments of epilepsy, were pleased with the panel's recommendation.

"This is a very good development, and it basically underscores that there are medicinal properties to some of the cannabinoids," said Dr. Igor Grant, director of the Center for Medicinal Cannabis Research at the University of California San Diego. "I think there could well be other cannabinoids that are of therapeutic use, but there is just not enough research on them to say."

The panel recommended approval of the drug to treat two rare forms of epilepsy — Lennox-Gastaut syndrome and Dravet syndrome.

They are among the most difficult types of epilepsy to treat, with nearly all patients continuing to have seizures despite currently available medications, according to the F.D.A. The large number of seizures — experts say a person can have multiple episodes a day — puts children at high risk for intellectual and developmental disabilities, as well as death. Lennox-Gastaut syndrome usually appears between ages 3 and 5, and Dravet syndrome earlier.

There are an estimated 30,000 children and adults with Lennox-Gastaut syndrome and fewer than that with Dravet syndrome. Because the conditions are so rare, GW Pharmaceuticals has received an orphan drug designation for Epidiolex.

"It's very important that we have additional treatments because these patients have very, very difficult to control seizures," said Dr. Jerzy P. Szaflarski, a neurology professor at the University of Alabama at Birmingham, who directs the university's epilepsy division. "I get questions about cannabidiol almost every day."

The briefing materials prepared for the committee by F.D.A. staff made it clear that the agency supports the application. The F.D.A. wrote that GW Pharma had submitted positive results of efficacy from three randomized, double-blind, placebo-controlled trials conducted in patients with both diseases.

"The statistically significant and clinically meaningful results from these three studies provide substantial evidence of the effectiveness of CBD for the treatment of seizures associated with LGS and DS," the agency noted.

The briefing papers also reported risk of a potentially serious side effect — liver injury — but said it could be managed.

Epidiolex would be the first of a new class of drugs to treat epilepsy. The F.D.A. is not bound by advisory committee recommendations but often follows them.

Christina SanInocencio, a nurse and founder of the LGS Foundation, hopes it does.

"I have a brother with the disorder," Ms. SanInocencio said. "I've met hundreds and hundreds of families who have kids living with it. It's so devastating. Any new medicine that comes to the market is a really big win for our community."

Surest Way to Face Marijuana Charges in New York: Be Black or Hispanic

BY BENJAMIN MUELLER, ROBERT GEBELOFF AND SAHIL CHINOY | MAY 13, 2018

The police explanation that more black and Hispanic people are arrested on marijuana charges because complaints are high in their neighborhoods doesn't hold up to scrutiny.

THEY SIT IN courtroom pews, almost all of them young black men, waiting their turn before a New York City judge to face a charge that no longer exists in some states: possessing marijuana. They tell of smoking in a housing project hallway, or of being in a car with a friend who was smoking, or of lighting up a Black & Mild cigar the police mistake for a blunt.

MARK ABRAMSON FOR THE NEW YORK TIMES

Pedestrians in the Greenpoint neighborhood of Brooklyn in April 2018. Greenpoint is largely a white neighborhood, and only 4 percent of the population is black.

There are many ways to be arrested on marijuana charges, but one pattern has remained true through years of piecemeal policy changes in New York: The primary targets are black and Hispanic people.

Across the city, black people were arrested on low-level marijuana charges at eight times the rate of white, non-Hispanic people over the past three years, The New York Times found. Hispanic people were arrested at five times the rate of white people. In Manhattan, the gap is even starker: Black people there were arrested at 15 times the rate of white people.

With crime dropping and the Police Department under pressure to justify the number of low-level arrests it makes, a senior police official recently testified to lawmakers that there was a simple reason for the racial imbalance: More residents in predominantly black and Hispanic neighborhoods were calling to complain about marijuana.

MARK ABRAMSON FOR THE NEW YORK TIMES

Canarsie's Rockaway Parkway bustled with activity last month. There are four times as many arrests for marijuana in the precinct that includes Canarsie, which is 85 percent black.

An analysis by The Times found that fact did not fully explain the racial disparity. Instead, among neighborhoods where people called about marijuana at the same rate, the police almost always made arrests at a higher rate in the area with more black residents, The Times found.

In Brooklyn, officers in the precinct covering Canarsie arrested people on marijuana possession charges at a rate more than four times as high as in the precinct that includes Greenpoint, despite residents calling 311, the city's help line, and 911 to complain about marijuana at the same rate, police data show. The Canarsie precinct is 85 percent black. The Greenpoint precinct is 4 percent black.

In Queens, the marijuana arrest rate is more than 10 times as high in the precinct covering Queens Village as it is in precinct that serves Forest Hills. Both got marijuana complaints at the same rate, but the Queens Village precinct is just over half black, while the one covering Forest Hills has a tiny portion of black residents.

And in Manhattan, officers in a precinct covering a stretch of western Harlem make marijuana arrests at double the rate of their counterparts in a precinct covering the northern part of the Upper West Side. Both received complaints at the same rate, but the precinct covering western Harlem has double the percentage of black residents as the one that serves the Upper West Side.

The Times's analysis, combined with interviews with defendants facing marijuana charges, lawyers and police officers, paints a picture of uneven enforcement. In some neighborhoods, officers expected by their commanders to be assertive on the streets seize on the smell of marijuana and stop people who are smoking. In others, people smoke in public without fear of an officer passing by or stopping them.

Black neighborhoods often contend with more violent crime, and the police often deploy extra officers there, which can lead to residents being exposed more to the police.

"More cops in neighborhoods means they're more likely to encounter somebody smoking," said Jeffrey Fagan, a Columbia Law

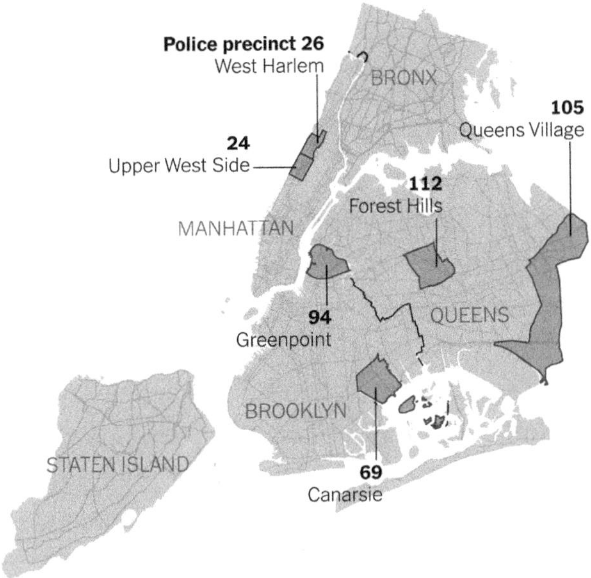

BY THE NEW YORK TIMES

School professor who also advised The Times on its marijuana-arrest analysis.

But more officers are historically assigned to black neighborhoods than would be expected based on crime rates, according to a study by Professor Fagan. And research has found "there is no good evidence" that marijuana arrests in New York City are associated with reductions in serious crime.

Officers who catch someone smoking marijuana are legally able to stop and search that person and check for open warrants. Some defense lawyers and criminologists say those searches and warrant checks are the real impetus for enforcing marijuana laws more heavily in some neighborhoods.

The analysis by The Times shows that at least some quality-of-life arrests have more to do with the Police Department's strategies than with residents who call for help, undermining one of the arguments the police have used to defend mass enforcement of minor offenses in an era of declining serious crime.

The analysis examined how marijuana arrests were related to the marijuana-complaint rate, race, violent-crime levels, the poverty rate and homeownership data in each precinct. It also considered the borough where an arrest took place to account for different policing practices across the city. The arrests represent cases in which the most serious charge against someone was low-level marijuana possession.

Government surveys have shown that black and white people use marijuana at roughly the same rate. Marijuana smoke wafts down streets all over the city, from the brownstones in upper-middle-class areas of Manhattan to apartment buildings in working-class neighborhoods in other boroughs.

Mayor Bill de Blasio said in late 2014 that the police would largely give summonses instead of making arrests for carrying personal marijuana, and reserve arrests mainly for smoking in public. Since then, the police have arrested 17,500 people for marijuana possession on average a year, down from about 26,000 people in 2014, and issued thousands of additional summonses. Overall, arrests have dropped sharply from their recent peak of more than 50,000 during some years under Mayor Michael R. Bloomberg.

About 87 percent of those arrested in recent years have been black or Hispanic, a proportion that has remained roughly the same for decades, according to research led by Harry G. Levine, a sociology professor at Queens College.

"What you have is people smoking weed in the same places in any neighborhood in the city," said Scott Levy, a special counsel to the criminal defense practice at the Bronx Defenders, who has studied marijuana arrests. "It's just those neighborhoods are patrolled very, very differently. And the people in those neighborhoods are seen very differently by the police."

Responding to The Times's analysis, the Police Department said pockets of violent crime — and the heavier deployments that result — push up marijuana arrests in some neighborhoods. J. Peter Donald,

MARK ABRAMSON FOR THE NEW YORK TIMES

A woman in the Forest Hills neighborhood of Queens, where the marijuana arrest rate in the precinct is far lower than it is in the precinct covering Queens Village, even though the number of 911 and 311 complaints about marijuana are about the same in each precinct.

an assistant commissioner in the department's public information office, also said more people smoke in public in some neighborhoods than others, driving up arrests. He said 911 and 311 complaints about marijuana had increased in recent years.

"N.Y.P.D. police officers enforce the law fairly and evenly, not only where and when they observe infractions but also in response to complaints from 911 and 311 calls, tenant associations, community councils and build-the-block meetings," Mr. Donald said in a statement.

Appearing before the City Council in February, Chief Dermot F. Shea said, "The remaining arrests that we make now are overlaid exactly in the parts of the city where we are receiving complaints from the public." He asked, "What would you have the police do when people are calling?"

Police data do show that neighborhoods with many black and Hispanic residents tend to generate more 311 and 911 complaints about marijuana. Criminal justice reform advocates said that is not because more people are smoking marijuana in those areas. Rather, people in poor neighborhoods call the police because they are less likely to have a responsive landlord, building superintendent or co-op board member who can field their complaints.

Rory Lancman, a councilman from Queens who pressed police officials for the marijuana data at the February hearing, said with the police still arresting thousands of people for smoking amid a widespread push for reform, the police "blame it on the communities themselves because they're the ones calling on us."

The city's 77 precincts, led by commanders with their own enforcement priorities, show erratic arrest patterns. In Sunset Park, Brooklyn, for example, the police made more than twice as many marijuana arrests last year as in 2016, despite receiving roughly the same number of annual complaints. And in a precinct covering a section of northwestern Harlem, arrests dropped to 90 last year from almost 700 a year earlier, even though complaints fell only slightly from one year to the next.

Criticism of marijuana arrests provided fuel for Mr. de Blasio's campaign for mayor in 2013, when he won promising to "reverse the racial impact of low-level marijuana arrests." The next year the new Brooklyn district attorney, Ken Thompson, defied the Police Department and said his office would stop prosecuting many low-level marijuana arrests.

Yet the disparities remain. Black and Hispanic people are the main targets of arrests even in mostly white neighborhoods. In the precinct covering the southern part of the Upper West Side, for example, white residents outnumber their black and Hispanic neighbors by six to one, yet seven out of every 10 people charged with marijuana possession in the last three years are black or Hispanic, state data show. In the precinct covering Park Slope, Brooklyn, where a fifth of the residents are black or Hispanic, three-quarters of those arrested on marijuana charges are black or Hispanic.

MARK ABRAMSON FOR THE NEW YORK TIMES

A pedestrian on Jamaica Avenue in Queens Village, where the marijuana arrest rate is more than 10 times as high as it is in Forest Hills.

The question of how to address those disparities has divided Democratic politicians in New York. Cynthia Nixon, who is campaigning for the Democratic nomination for governor against Gov. Andrew M. Cuomo, has vowed to legalize marijuana and clear people's arrest records. Mr. de Blasio and Mr. Cuomo have been reluctant to support the same measures.

In Criminal Court in Brooklyn on a recent Monday, the people waiting in the crowded pews to be arraigned on marijuana charges were almost all black men. In interviews, some declined to give their full names for fear of compounding the consequences of their arrests.

They had missed work or school, sometimes losing hundreds of dollars in wages, to show up in court — often twice, because paperwork was not ready the first time. Their cases were all dismissed so long as they stayed out of trouble for a stretch, an indication of what Scott Hechinger, a senior staff lawyer and director of policy at Brooklyn

Defender Services, said was the low value the court system places on such cases.

Eli, 18, said he had been smoking in a housing project hallway because his parents preferred him to keep it out of the apartment. Greg, 39, said he had not even been smoking himself, but was sitting in his car next to his wife, who he said smokes marijuana to relieve the symptoms of multiple sclerosis.

"They do it because that's the easiest way to arrest you," Greg said.

Rashawn Nicol, 27, said officers found his female friend holding a lit blunt on a third-floor stairwell landing in a Brooklyn housing project. They backed off arresting her once she started crying, he said, but said they needed to bring their supervisor an arrest because he had radioed over a noise complaint. "Somebody's got to go down for this," Mr. Nicol said an officer told him. So they let her go, but arrested him.

Several people asked why the police hound residents for small-time infractions like marijuana in more violent neighborhoods, but are slow to follow up about serious crimes. "The resources they waste for this are ridiculous," Mr. Nicol said.

Canadians Brace for Cultural Changes as Marijuana Becomes Legal

BY DAN BILEFSKY AND CATHERINE PORTER | JUNE 20, 2018

MONTREAL — For one of Canada's largest legal cannabis companies, the vote in Parliament this week to legalize recreational marijuana use represents a broad opportunity to develop new products, including marijuana infused drinks.

The hope, said Adam Greenblatt, a manager with the company, Canopy Growth, "is that in five years time people will be drinking cannabis drinks at a cocktail party as if drinking a good wine."

Matteo Rossant, 21, a business graduate at Concordia University in Montreal, also envisions an expansive future, one in which he sells maple syrup, lollipops and jelly treats made with cannabis.

COLE BURSTON FOR THE NEW YORK TIMES

Trees Station, an illegal marijuana dispensary in Toronto, has avoided being shut down. It has presented itself as if it were a medical dispensary.

But Rémi Letendre, 81, a retired Quebec radio host, worries that legal marijuana sales and consumption will leave cities like Toronto and Montreal overrun by stoned adolescents and marijuana tourists from the United States stumbling around the sidewalks.

People across Canada were grappling on Wednesday with the legalization of recreational marijuana, which represents one of the most sweeping changes in Canadian culture in decades.

Many questions remain, including whether law enforcement will be able to tame a vibrant black market for cannabis that has been thriving in the shadows and whether consumers will reject smoking government-approved joints.

The Liberal government of Prime Minister Justin Trudeau had argued that legalization was necessary to eliminate an illegal cannabis industry estimated to be worth as much as $7 billion a year and to protect young people from the risks of illegal drugs. The law will go into effect on Oct. 17, Mr. Trudeau said Wednesday, to give provinces time to get their retail systems running.

But proponents of marijuana legalization may face an unlikely challenge: customers who worry that government-approved products will take some of the thrill out of pot smoking.

Tristan Peloquin, a Montreal-based author of a soon-to-be-published book, "The Little Green Book of Cannabis: A Survival Guide," predicted that veteran consumers would come around.

"Smoking pot has long been a rebellious anti-government activity," he said, "but some of the illegal stuff has pesticides and pot smokers will ultimately want better quality pot."

The Quebec Cannabis Company, the new provincial marijuana monopoly, has been examining how to sell cannabis, given restrictions that, for example, forbid glamorizing it in marketing or selling it in glass display cases behind a counter.

Mathieu Gaudreault, a spokesman for the company, said customers might be able to at least smell the marijuana, which will be sold in sealed sachets, "as if they were smelling perfume." Customers will be

COLE BURSTON FOR THE NEW YORK TIMES

Kerri MacDonald, an employee at Hotbox Cafe, a smoking lounge and shop in Toronto's Kensington Market.

asked for identification at the entrance to retail stores to prove that they are at least 18 years old, the legal age for buying alcohol and cannabis in Quebec.

At the official stores, one gram will cost about $6; other products will be offered, both at stores and online, with different degrees of potency.

While Canadians will soon be allowed to smoke and sell marijuana with impunity for the first time in 95 years, hundreds of illegal dispensaries have already popped up across the country, underlining the challenges the government and law enforcement will face.

Trees Station, one of many illegal pot dispensaries in Toronto's bohemian Kensington Market, has been open for two years, selling more than 30 different kinds of marijuana, with names like Pink Cinderella and Organic Charlotte's Web.

The drug is offered in capsules and extract form, too. Customers can buy THC lip balm and a canine calming cannabis powder called

COLE BURSTON FOR THE NEW YORK TIMES

The products on display at a Toronto marijuana dispensary.

Calm and Quiet. Business is so good, the owners have no intention of shutting down when the new law goes into effect in October. Instead, they have plans to open two new sites.

"We're going to keep on doing what we're doing," said Nathan Murdock, the store manager.

The store presents itself as if it were a medical dispensary. There is a green cross on a signboard on the street outside and a note on the door that warns buyers that they need to show an ID, as they would at an authorized dispensary.

But it is just a pretense. Inside, the staff serves a continual line of shoppers from behind a glass counter, sorting through their orders wearing latex gloves.

Although Canada legalized medical marijuana in 2001, and today patients must order marijuana by mail from producers licensed by the government, hundreds of black market dispensaries have proliferated.

On Wednesday afternoon, Eartha Masek-Kelly, a 21-year-old musician, bought a quarter of an ounce of Green House Ocean Grown Kush from the counter as she had done every other day for the past year to calm her anxiety and depression.

"Why put resources into shutting down independent retailers that are just helping people?" she asked.

In effort to rein in illegal dispensaries, Ontario has passed tough laws allowing the police to shut them down. But as quickly as some illegal stores have been shut down, others have opened up.

Staff Sgt. Lesley Hildred of the Toronto Police said officers took the door off one of the closed dispensaries to ensure that it could not reopen quickly. "It takes a lot of police hours," the sergeant said. "We can't be there enforcing the law all the time. I have other things to do."

Mr. Peloquin said that some legal medical marijuana growers had been selling their surplus crop to illegal sites that peddle marijuana online.

"There is a massive gray market already and the police know it exists," he said. "But if they arrest someone and a person shows they are a designated producer, it is hard to prove criminal intent. So it is very hard to clamp down on this."

Gérard Deltell, an opposition Conservative member of the federal Parliament from Quebec City, argued that the government had rushed to legalize marijuana before law enforcement in some provinces were ready. He predicted that organized crime would continue to hold sway.

"It is shocking that the Canadian government wants to become the pot dealer for the nation," he said.

Mr. Letendre, the retired radio host, offered perhaps the most dire vision of what legalization might produce. "Young people from all over the world will come to smoke weed in Montreal, and we will soon become a country of potheads," he said as he rode his electric scooter through downtown Montreal.

But other people, especially young ones, view legalization as an enormous business prospect.

Mr. Rossant, 21, the recent university graduate, is starting a marijuana lifestyle magazine called Maples. He also wants to produce a variety of maple-derived, marijuana-infused products, and he is hoping that the law will be liberalized as demand grows.

"For a young entrepreneur like me, the pot industry feels easier to get into than the tech sector," he said. "Besides, we millennials have the know-how when it comes to the pot-market — we have all smoked pot."

DAN BILEFSKY reported from Montreal, and **CATHERINE PORTER** from Toronto. **JASMIN LAVOIE** and **IAN AUSTEN** contributed reporting from Ottawa.

Glossary

amphetamine A drug (often used illicitly) that acts as a stimulant, causing the nervous system to be more active, providing energy and mental excitement.

appropriation Funds set aside for a specific purpose.

athwart Across.

barbiturate A drug (often used illicitly) that acts as a depressant, causing a sedative or hypnotic effect.

beatnik A member of the countercultural movement of the 1950s and '60s that rejected societal mores and embraced cannabis use.

cannabis indica A species of the Cannabis genus commonly known as marijuana often cultivated for medical, recreational and industrial use.

cannabis sativa A species of the Cannabis genus commonly known as marijuana often cultivated for medical, recreational and industrial use.

capsaicin A component of hot peppers that gives them their hot flavor.

cognoscente An expert or connoisseur on a particular subject.

deleterious Harmful.

gas chromatography A process in which a sample mixture is vaporized and injected into a stream of gas so that it will be separated into distinct components.

gewgaw A trinket or trifle.

haloperidol A depressant of the central nervous system used as an antipsychotic drug.

Harrison Act A U.S. federal law passed in 1914 that taxed the production and importation of opiates and coca products.

hashish The resin of the flowering female Cannabis plants smoked or ingested for its intoxicating effect.

hemp Common name for the Cannabis sativa plant often used industrially as a fiber.

insidious Simultaneously harmful, yet enticing.

laxity The quality or state of being not stringent or lax.

lethargy The quality or state of being sluggish or abnormally drowsy.

mass spectrometry A method for identifying the chemical makeup of a substance.

mete To distribute by measure.

milieu The social environment or physical setting in which something develops.

opiate A drug derived from opium that acts as a pain reliever and induces sleep.

pernicious Highly destructive, deadly.

phencyclidine A drug primarily used in veterinary science as an anesthetic and illicitly by humans as a psychedelic drug.

Schedule I A category of drugs, as defined by the Controlled Substances Act, deemed to have no recognized medical use.

slovenliness The quality of being untidy or unkempt in personal appearance or hygiene.

vagabondage The condition of one who wanders with no fixed home.

Media Literacy Terms

"Media literacy" refers to the ability to access, understand, critically assess and create media. The following terms are important components of media literacy, and they will help you critically engage with the articles in this title.

angle The aspect of a news story that a journalist focuses on and develops.

attribution The method by which a source is identified or by which facts and information are assigned to the person who provided them.

balance Principle of journalism that both perspectives of an argument should be presented in a fair way.

bias A disposition of prejudice in favor of a certain idea, person or perspective.

byline Name of the writer, usually placed between the headline and the story.

caption Identifying copy for a picture; also called a legend or cutline.

commentary A type of story that is an expression of opinion on recent events by a journalist generally known as a commentator.

credibility The quality of being trustworthy and believable, said of a journalistic source.

critical review A type of story that describes an event or work of art, such as a theater performance, film, concert, book, restaurant, radio or television program, exhibition or musical piece, and offers critical assessment of its quality and reception.

editorial Article of opinion or interpretation.

human interest story A type of story that focuses on individuals and how events or issues affect their life, generally offering a sense of relatability to the reader.

impartiality Principle of journalism that a story should not reflect a journalist's bias and should contain balance.

intention The motive or reason behind something, such as the publication of a news story.

interview story A type of story in which the facts are gathered primarily by interviewing another person or persons.

motive The reason behind something, such as the publication of a news story or a source's perspective on an issue.

news story An article or style of expository writing that reports news, generally in a straightforward fashion and without editorial comment.

op-ed An opinion piece that reflects a prominent individual's opinion on a topic of interest.

paraphrase The summary of an individual's words, with attribution, rather than a direct quotation of their exact words.

quotation The use of an individual's exact words indicated by the use of quotation marks and proper attribution.

reliability The quality of being dependable and accurate, said of a journalistic source.

rhetorical device Technique in writing intending to persuade the reader or communicate a message from a certain perspective.

style A distinctive use of language in writing or speech; also a news or publishing organization's rules for consistent use of language with regards to spelling, punctuation, typography and capitalization, usually regimented by a house style guide.

tone A manner of expression in writing or speech.

Media Literacy Questions

1. Identify the sources cited in the article "Poison Put in Cigarettes" (on page 10). How does the journalist attribute information to each of these sources in the article? Do these sources offer a variety of perspectives on the issue?

2. The article "Marijuana Smoking Is Reported Safe" (on page 17) cites a variety of sources. Identify several direct quotes and paraphrases throughout the article. What are the strengths of the use of a direct quote as opposed to a paraphrase? What are the weaknesses?

3. The article "Quotas" (on page 25) is an example of a letter to the editor. What are letters to the editor? What do you feel are their journalistic value?

4. What is the value of the photographs published with the article "City Seeks to Kill Marijuana Weeds" (on page 37)?

5. For the article "Narcotics a Growing Problem of Affluent Youth" (on page 40), Martin Arnold interviewed various sources. What value do these interviews contribute to the story?

6. James L. Goddard's piece "Marihuana Reconsidered" (on page 81) is an example of a critical review. What is the purpose of a critical review? Do you feel this article achieved that purpose?

7. What type of story is "New Parental Push Against Marijuana" (on page 101)? Can you identify another article in this collection that is the same type of story?

8. Compare Harold M. Schmeck Jr.'s 1979 article "Research on Marijuana Finds Many Risks, Some Benefits" (on page 96) with Philip J. Hilts's 1990 article "Scientists Learn How Marijuana Works in Brain" (on page 136). How do these two articles differ in perspective? What new information was discovered between the publication of the first article and the second?

9. The article "Misguided Marijuana War" (on page 152) is an example of an editorial. Identify how The New York Times Editorial Board's attitude and tone help convey their opinion on the topic.

10. "A Perplexing Marijuana Side Effect Relieved by Hot Showers" (on page 186) is an example of a human interest story. What is the purpose of a human interest story? How well does this article achieve that purpose?

11. What is the intention of the article "Surest Way to Face Marijuana Charges in New York: Be Black or Hispanic" (on page 194)? How effectively does it achieve its intended purpose?

Citations

All citations in this list are formatted according to the Modern Language Association's (MLA) style guide.

BOOK CITATION

NEW YORK TIMES EDITORIAL STAFF, THE. *Marijuana.* New York: New York Times Educational Publishing, 2019.

ONLINE ARTICLE CITATIONS

APPLE, R.W., JR. "Four G.I.'s Are Accused of Possessing Narcotics, 20 Under Inquiry." *The New York Times,* 27 Jan. 1966, https://www.nytimes.com/1966/01/27/archives/four-gis-are-accused-of-possessing-narcotics-20-under-inquiry-4-gis.html.

ARNOLD, MARTIN. "Narcotics a Growing Problem of Affluent Youth." *The New York Times,* 4 Jan. 1965, https://www.nytimes.com/1965/01/04/archives/narcotics-a-growing-problem-of-affluent-youth-beginning-with.html.

BILEFSKY, DAN, AND CATHERINE PORTER. "Canadians Brace for Cultural Changes as Marijuana Becomes Legal." *The New York Times,* 20 Jun. 2018, https://www.nytimes.com/2018/06/20/world/canada/canada-marijuana-legalize.html.

BOYD, GERALD M. "Bush, Citing Cost, Says Drug War Will Focus Largely on Education." *The New York Times,* 26 Jan. 1989, https://www.nytimes.com/1989/01/26/us/bush-citing-cost-says-drug-war-will-focus-largely-on-education.html.

BRINKLEY, JOEL. "Anti-Drug Law: Words, Deeds, Political Expediency." *The New York Times,* 27 Oct. 1986, https://www.nytimes.com/1986/10/27/us/anti-drug-law-words-deeds-political-expediency.html.

BROOKE, JAMES. "5 States Vote Medical Use of Marijuana." *The New York Times,* 5 Nov. 1998, https://www.nytimes.com/1998/11/05/us/the-1998-elections-the-states-drug-policy-5-states-vote-medical-use-of-marijuana.html.

COLEMAN BRYNNER, ELISABETH. "New Parental Push Against Marijuana." *The New York Times,* 10 Feb. 1980, https://www.nytimes.com/1980/02/10/archives/new-parental-push-against-marijuana-marijuana.html.

CORRY, JOHN. "Drugs a Growing Campus Problem." *The New York Times,* 21 Mar. 1966, https://www.nytimes.com/1966/03/21/archives/drugs-a-growing-campus-problem-the-use-of-drugs-on-college-campuses.html.

DE COURCY, JOSEPH. "Mexico to Join U.S. in Fight on Drugs." *The New York Times,* 10 May 1925, https://www.nytimes.com/1925/05/10/archives/mexico-to-join-us-in-fight-on-drugs-treaty-is-expected-to-cut-down.html.

FREUDENHEIM, MILT. "Booming Business: Drug Use Tests." *The New York Times,* 3 Jan. 1990, https://www.nytimes.com/1990/01/03/business/booming-business-drug-use-tests.html.

FULLER, THOMAS. "Recreational Pot Is Officially Legal in California." *The New York Times,* 1 Jan. 2018, https://www.nytimes.com/2018/01/01/us/legal-pot-california.html.

GODDARD, JAMES L. "Marihuana Reconsidered." *The New York Times,* 27 Jun. 1971, https://www.nytimes.com/1971/06/27/archives/marihuana-reconsidered-by-lester-grinspoon-m-d-443-pp-cambridge.html.

GOETHE, C. M. "Quotas." *The New York Times,* 15 Sept. 1935, https://www.nytimes.com/1935/09/15/archives/quotas.html.

GOLDBERG, CAREY. "Medical Marijuana Use Winning Backing." *The New York Times,* 30 Oct. 1996, https://www.nytimes.com/1996/10/30/us/medical-marijuana-use-winning-backing.html.

GOLDEN, STEPHEN A. O. "Police Look On as Hippies Stage a Park Smoke-In." *The New York Times,* 31 Jul. 1967, https://www.nytimes.com/1967/07/31/archives/police-look-on-as-hippies-stage-a-park-smokein.html.

GREENHOUSE, LINDA. "Justices Say U.S. May Prohibit the Use of Medical Marijuana." *The New York Times,* 7 Jun. 2005, https://www.nytimes.com/2005/06/07/politics/justices-say-us-may-prohibit-the-use-of-medical-marijuana.html.

HEALY, JACK. "Up Early and in Line for a Marijuana Milestone in Colorado." *The New York Times,* 1 Jan. 2014, https://www.nytimes.com/2014/01/02/us/colorado-stores-throw-open-their-doors-to-pot-buyers.html.

HILTS, PHILIP J. "Scientists Learn How Marijuana Works in Brain." *The New York Times,* 21 Jul. 1990, https://www.nytimes.com/1990/07/21/us/scientists-learn-how-marijuana-works-in-brain.html.

JOHNSON, KIRK. "Still-Divided Washington Prepares for Start of Recreational

Marijuana Sales." *The New York Times*, 6 Jul. 2014, https://www.nytimes .com/2014/07/07/us/07potshop.html.

KAPLAN, SHEILA. "F.D.A. Panel Recommends Approval of Cannabis-Based Drug for Epilepsy." *The New York Times*, 19 Apr. 2018, https://www .nytimes.com/2018/04/19/health/epidiolex-fda-cannabis-marajuana.html.

KIFNER, JOHN. "The Drug Scene: Many Students Now Regard Marijuana as a Part of Growing Up." *The New York Times*, 11 Jan. 1968, https://www .nytimes.com/1968/01/11/archives/the-drug-scene-many-students-now -regard-marijuana-as-a-part-of.html.

KRAUSS, CLIFFORD. "Canada to Offer Marijuana to Medical Patients." *The New York Times*, 10 Jul. 2003, https://www.nytimes.com/2003/07/10/world /canada-to-offer-marijuana-to-medical-patients.html.

MUELLER, BENJAMIN, ET AL. "Surest Way to Face Marijuana Charges in New York: Be Black or Hispanic." *The New York Times*, 13 May 2018, https:// www.nytimes.com/2018/05/13/nyregion/marijuana-arrests-nyc-race.html.

THE NEW YORK TIMES. "City Seeks to Kill Marijuana Weeds." *The New York Times*, 20 Jun. 1951, https://www.nytimes.com/1951/06/20/archives/city -seeks-to-kill-marijuana-weeds-locating-and-destroying.html.

THE NEW YORK TIMES. " 'Decriminalizing' Marijuana." *The New York Times*, 20 Feb. 1972, https://www.nytimes.com/1972/02/20/archives/-decriminalizing -marijuana.html.

THE NEW YORK TIMES. "Experts Discount Marijuana as Big Factor in Crime but Drive on It Will Be Pressed." *The New York Times*, 12 Jan. 1945, https:// www.nytimes.com/1945/01/12/archives/experts-discount-marijuana-as-big -factor-in-crime-but-drive-on-if.html.

THE NEW YORK TIMES. "High Court Backs Tax on Marihuana." *The New York Times*, 14 Nov. 1950, https://www.nytimes.com/1950/11/14/archives/high -court-backs-tax-on-marihuana-but-tribunal-agrees-levy-of-100-a.html.

THE NEW YORK TIMES. "House Group Votes Jail in Drug Cases." *The New York Times*, 16 Jun. 1951, https://www.nytimes.com/1951/06/16/archives/house -group-votes-jail-in-drug-cases-mandatory-minimum-terms.html.

THE NEW YORK TIMES. "Marijuana as Medicine." *The New York Times*, 17 Jul. 1978, https://www.nytimes.com/1978/07/17/archives/marijuana-as -medicine.html.

THE NEW YORK TIMES. "Marijuana as Medicine." *The New York Times*, 27 Aug. 1983, https://www.nytimes.com/1983/08/27/opinion/no-headline-127781. html.

THE NEW YORK TIMES. "Marijuana Smoking Is Reported Safe." *The New York Times,* 21 Nov. 1926, https://www.nytimes.com/1926/11/21/archives/marijuana-smoking-is-reported-safe-hemp-leaves-classed-in-some.html.

THE NEW YORK TIMES. "Marijuana Traffic Is on the Increase." *The New York Times,* 31 Jan. 1945, https://www.nytimes.com/1945/01/31/archives/marijuana-traffic-is-on-the-increase-this-city-is-focal-point-says.html.

THE NEW YORK TIMES. "Misguided Marijuana War." *The New York Times,* 4 Feb. 2003, https://www.nytimes.com/2003/02/04/opinion/misguided-marijuana-war.html.

THE NEW YORK TIMES. "Pentagon Steps Up Fight on Drug Use in Vietnam." *The New York Times,* 16 Feb. 1968, https://www.nytimes.com/1968/02/16/archives/pentagon-steps-up-fight-on-drug-use-in-vietnam-sharp-rise-noted-in.html.

THE NEW YORK TIMES. "Poison Put in Cigarettes." *The New York Times,* 10 May 1914, https://www.nytimes.com/1914/05/10/archives/article-7-no-title.html.

THE NEW YORK TIMES."Use of Marijuana Spreading in West." *The New York Times,* 16 Sept. 1934, https://www.nytimes.com/1934/09/16/archives/use-of-marijuana-spreading-in-west-poisonous-weed-is-being-sold.html.

THE NEW YORK TIMES."War on Marijuana Urged on Parents." *The New York Times,* 4 May 1937, https://www.nytimes.com/1937/05/04/archives/war-on-marihuana-urged-on-parents-federal-expert-calls-on-pta.html.

PASSELL, PETER. "The High Hidden Costs of the War on Marijuana." *The New York Times,* 5 Sept. 1989, https://www.nytimes.com/1989/09/05/us/economic-watch-the-high-hidden-costs-of-the-war-on-marijuana.html.

RABIN, RONI CARYN. "Legalizing of Marijuana Raises Health Concerns." *The New York Times,* 7 Jan. 2013, https://well.blogs.nytimes.com/2013/01/07/legalizing-of-marijuana-raises-health-concerns/.

RABIN, RONI CARYN. "A Perplexing Marijuana Side Effect Relieved by Hot Showers." *The New York Times,* 5 Apr. 2018, https://www.nytimes.com/2018/04/05/well/a-perplexing-marijuana-side-effect-relieved-by-hot-showers.html.

REINHOLD, ROBERT R. "Marijuana Held a Public Hazard." *The New York Times,* 26 Sept. 1967, https://www.nytimes.com/1967/09/26/archives/marijuana-held-a-public-hazard-psychiatrist-links-drug-to-a-rise-in.html.

SCHLOSSER, ERIC. "The World: Up in Smoke; The U.S. Bucks a Trend on Marijuana Laws." *The New York Times,* 1 Jun. 2003, https://www.nytimes.com/2003/06/01/weekinreview/the-world-up-in-smoke-the-us-bucks-a

-trend-on-marijuana-laws.html.

SCHMECK, HAROLD M., JR. "Research on Marijuana Finds Many Risks, Some Benefits." *The New York Times*, 9 Oct. 1979, https://www.nytimes.com/1979/10/09/archives/research-on-marijuana-finds-many-risks-some-benefits-marijuana-many.html.

STOUT, DAVID, AND SOLOMON MOORE. "U.S. Won't Prosecute in States That Allow Medical Marijuana." *The New York Times*, 19 Oct. 2009, https://www.nytimes.com/2009/10/20/us/20cannabis.html.

SULLIVAN, WALTER. "Marijuana Study by U.S. Finds No Serious Harm." *The New York Times*, 9 Jul. 1975, https://www.nytimes.com/1975/07/09/archives/marijuana-study-by-us-finds-no-serious-harm.html.

TREASTER, JOSEPH B. "Costly and Scarce, Marijuana Is a High More Are Rejecting." *The New York Times*, 29 Oct. 1991, https://www.nytimes.com/1991/10/29/nyregion/costly-and-scarce-marijuana-is-a-high-more-are-rejecting.html.

TREASTER, JOSEPH B. "Doctors in Survey Support Marijuana Use by Cancer Patients." *The New York Times*, 1 May 1990, https://www.nytimes.com/1991/05/01/us/doctors-in-survey-support-marijuana-use-by-cancer-patients.html.

Index

This book is current up until the time of printing. For the most up-to-date reporting, visit www.nytimes.com.